The
Center
of the
Star

Understanding and Changing
the US Healthcare System

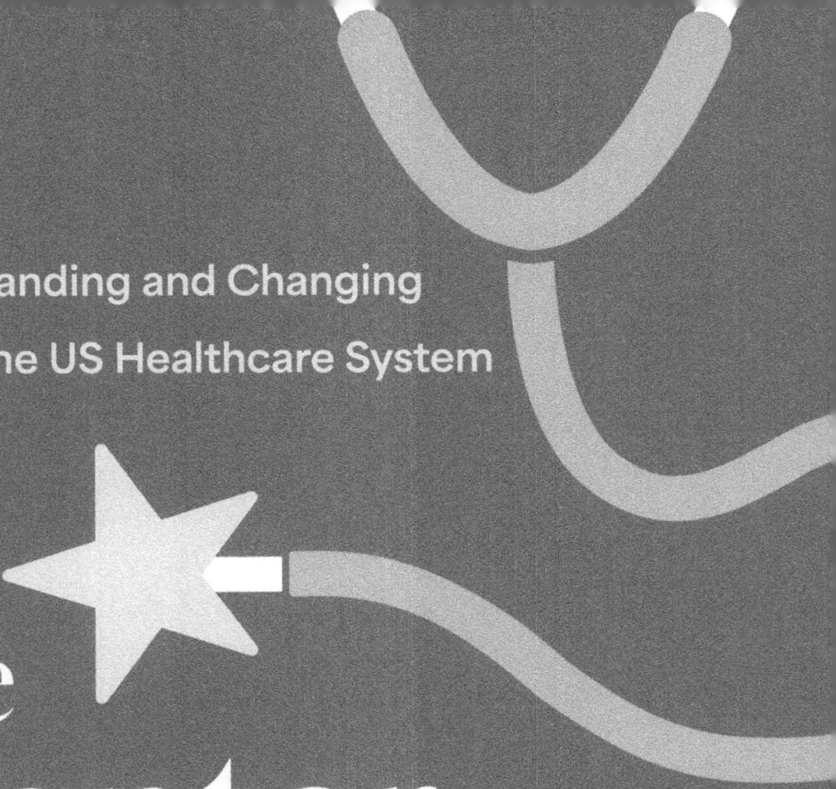

The Center of the Star

Judith Kunisch

Advantage | Books

Published by Advantage Books, Charleston, South Carolina.
An imprint of Advantage Media.

ADVANTAGE is a registered trademark, and the Advantage colophon is a trademark of Advantage Media Group, Inc.

Printed in the United States of America.

10 9 8 7 6 5 4 3 2 1

ISBN: 979-8-89188-263-8 (Paperback)
ISBN: 979-8-89188-264-5 (eBook)

Library of Congress Control Number: 2025906562

Cover design by Matthew Morse.
Layout design by Ruthie Wood.

This publication is designed to provide accurate and authoritative information in regard to the subject matter covered. It is sold with the understanding that the publisher is not engaged in rendering legal, accounting, or other professional services. If legal advice or other expert assistance is required, the services of a competent professional person should be sought.

Advantage Books is an imprint of Advantage Media Group. Advantage Media helps busy entrepreneurs, CEOs, and leaders write and publish a book to grow their business and become the authority in their field. Advantage authors comprise an exclusive community of industry professionals, idea-makers, and thought leaders. For more information go to **advantagemedia.com**.

In honor of Walt, who told me, "Keep Your Eye on the Star Always!"

CONTENTS

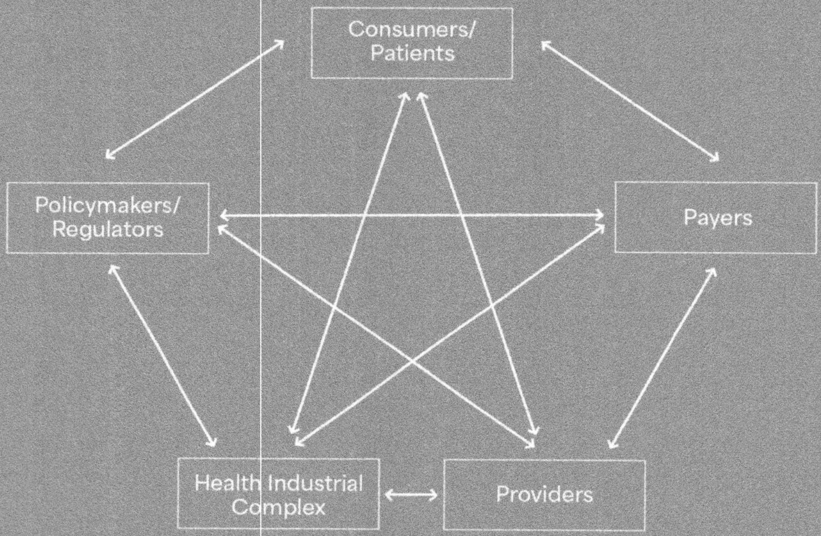

Consumers/
Patients
Policymakers/
Regulators
Payers
Health Industrial
Complex
Providers

INTRODUCTION
Systems Thinking

I was concluding a lecture on the US health system that focused on the five key sectors of consumers/patients, payers, providers, the health industrial complex (HIC), and policymakers/regulators. Behind me was a slide that displayed the healthcare system star framework, and before me sat an audience of a hundred healthcare providers, most of whom were relatively new to the profession. The majority were from the United States, and they represented diverse regions across the country.

As soon as I stopped talking, the questions and challenge statements came fast and furious. Someone raised a hand in the back of the room, then another shot up, and then another. "I heard that the US healthcare system should not be an economic entity," one said. "Yes, healthcare is a right and should be free for all," another added. "The time has come to make major changes or simply eliminate the system," a third person stated. Of course, this system was the very one I'd spent the previous forty-five minutes describing.

"Hmmm, interesting ideas," I said as I processed what to say next. I'd heard these objections many times before, and whenever I did, what became clear to me was that while everyone wanted change, most had little idea *how* the US health system worked. This meant the challenges and changes they suggested might alter or eliminate something that already worked well.

On the one hand, I couldn't blame them. Most people live busy lives, and even if they work in it, they do not think much about the *overall* system. They are generally aware of its local presence in their communities and their individual relationships with the health community. At the same time, their attention is regularly drawn to the issues of the larger health system by the media and by elected officials, who focus on such problems.

These problems include high costs for care and prescription drugs, socioeconomic and racial health disparities, inconsistent insurance coverages, rules concerning which providers can be used and paid for, medical debt, and more. Unfortunately, this list of items creates a perspective that there is *always* a problem. And frankly, most people don't want problems.

They want health, well-being, respect, good relationships with providers, and proper care when necessary. They want access to care and a source that pays for it. When a person needs to pay for care and cannot tap into either private or public sources, there can be an access problem. And people want lower healthcare costs.

If you are reading this book, you may be curious about how the healthcare system works. You may also be reading because you are involved with the system as a result of your job in one of the five sectors associated with healthcare. Or you may be reading because you want to make a change in the US health system. Even if you have nothing to do with the healthcare system daily, you may believe the system needs to change. But first, for everyone, no matter the reason to change the system, understanding it is critical. And understanding the structure and the dynamics is the key.

The health system is a very present part of our lives. We drive by hospitals and nursing homes on our way to work. We have friends who work in healthcare. We go to routine checkups or need a health form completed for our loved ones. And we see coverage of the health system through the media.

Thanks to these day-to-day experiences and our natural skew, this interpretation of healthcare is most often on a personal level. It's all about *me, my* family, *my* friends, *my* community, and *my* job. This can prevent us from recognizing the sheer size and complexity of the healthcare industry.

With all these thoughts at the forefront of my mind, I returned to my lecture and pointed to the framework on the screen to address the concerns raised. Years before, I'd created the star framework because I wanted to make effective change. I needed to know all the associated sectors and how they operated and related to each other.

The star framework lays out the five major sectors, which are necessary to run the US health system. They are all interrelated. The more I learned, the more I began to think not just about how each sector differed from the others but also about the interrelatedness of the sectors and the health system overall. This type of approach is a systems thinking perspective, and once I developed this way of thinking, I was never the same.

To the attendees in the room, I explained each sector and demonstrated how the arrows between them functioned. Since all the attendees were connected to the providers arm, I began by focusing on that area. Then, focusing on each sector's function, I pointed to the payers arm of the framework, with insurance companies and government payers being the most apparent components, followed by the policymaking arm, which regulates the entire system. Then, I turned to the HIC, which conducts and produces some of the most advanced medical research science in the world. Finally, I drew their eyes to the consumers/patients arm, which we're all a part of as we all eventually show up as patients or consumers.

I stressed to the attendees that while each of these is a discrete sector, *all* are interdependent. I emphasized the systems thinking perspective I had come to recognize as essential for the health system industry to operate. I explained how the star framework, and what it represents, enables leaders and people interested in making change to see the entire industry as an interdependent system and to use this as a basis to innovate change and ultimately affect outcomes. I added that if they failed to understand what each sector did and how all five sectors affected one another, even the best change efforts could fail.

Working to make a change only in one sector while ignoring the others and the relationships between all five would eventually lead to collapse. Why? Because in order to make effective changes in the US health system, we need to employ systems thinking. That is, thinking across and about all five sectors of the star and their interdependence.

Systems thinking (Burton, 2022; Meadows, 2008) is a way to view the makeup and workings of a large and diverse organization— such as industries, governments, or healthcare systems. When you reside in or are promoting a change in a specific sector, it's often hard to imagine why people from other sectors might be interested in something you consider your domain or specialty area.

Yet they may be interested for a whole host of reasons you may have never considered. They might be thinking about how the change will be financed, how it meets regulatory criteria, or how it can actually be delivered in the patient examining room. Understanding systems thinking is essential for managing and making changes in any complex system. Change within any complex and diverse system is almost always accompanied by disruption and conflict. As Mark

Gerzon (2006, p. 81) writes, "Systems thinking is identifying all (or as many as possible) of the significant elements related to conflict and understanding the relationship between them."

We address disruption by identifying what might be affected or upturned. Within healthcare, we do this by looking across all five sectors to determine how the change will affect each sector. When we use this approach, our thinking becomes more holistic, and we gain an understanding of the larger whole. We can identify impacts and differences, seeing a situation in an entirely novel way, a way that is both intriguing and engaging. With this viewpoint, we can make change that is effective and minimally disruptive across the sectors in the star framework.

And believe me, because we need to make changes in our healthcare system, we need people across the system who are positioned and able to make those changes. We need individuals with vision and creativity who want to understand the system and make lasting changes. These are our influencers. People who may already be thinking systemically and strategically within their sector and who recognize they must also think outside their sector to get the necessary sustainable results. These are our systems thinkers who can negotiate, operate, and affect outcomes within the system.

Add to this other people who know the healthcare system is complex yet need to know where to begin to make changes. Or people who have seen a change start and, after some period, see it fade away. People working in the system, using the system, governing the population, and being responsible for the general welfare of that population, all from their individual perspectives, see a need for change. People like you.

What makes me the right person to write this book? First, I have spent a lifetime exploring and experiencing the realities of healthcare economics, human rights, equity, policy, and other actualities while delivering healthcare in this country. I've participated in and led major healthcare system changes, which have involved working with the five sectors. I have mentored healthcare system leaders who have a passion for making healthcare change. My strong belief in paying it forward has led me to commit to sharing my knowledge and experience with you, inspiring and motivating you to join the cause for positive change in healthcare.

Like many lecture attendees offering up their revolutionary ideas, I began my healthcare system career at the bedside, giving patient care. However, I then stepped away from the bedside and moved on to leadership and executive positions in clinical services, managed care, and insurance. This is where I learned about the healthcare system in its entirety through having to develop a systems thinking approach.

These experiences, among others, provided valuable opportunities to work with and learn from other healthcare providers, lawyers, government policymakers, insurers, actuaries, Big Pharma, informaticists, and consumers and patients. I held these various positions and worked with many people across the healthcare system to make changes. I had the opportunity to think of the healthcare system from perspectives other than those unique to my particular sector.

I learned about the system's structure, its dynamics, the critical success factors for clinical services, and financial viability and regulatory requirements. I saw these factors play out in real time. I learned about the HIC and its significant contributions to healthcare in the US and abroad. And I have always understood the importance of keeping the consumers and patients as healthcare's north star because they are the people the system is designed to serve.

These collective thoughts prompted me to shift my thinking to the center of that star framework, and I began to think of change from a healthcare systems perspective—the system you will read about in this book and in which we want to see change.

If a systems thinking perspective is considered in any change plan, sustainable success is more likely, as is a resultant cost-effective system. If systems thinking is not considered in the change plan, the intended change and outcome can derail, and its costs might easily spiral out of control, leading to a fiscally unsustainable system called "chaos." This systems thinking perspective helps us work together to make a difference so true change can begin.

In part 1, I describe the system background and how we got to the system we have today. In part 2, I use the star framework to explain the sectors and to position ourselves to think across this extensive system. We need to think about the system as an interconnected whole by understanding each of its parts. In part 3, I describe the interplay and dynamics between the sectors and the largest change areas we are dealing with. All of this is to help you think and work from the star's center to create sustainable change.

What thinking from the star's center does not let us do is dismantle the system and start over. Instead, it helps us recognize what is at stake in each sector and how to play to each sector's strengths to get the best out of our system. Ultimately, everyone in every sector has the same overall goals. Almost no one gets up in the morning saying, "Today, I am going to give low-quality service, ignore the breadth of humanity in a human-focused industry, and see how much money we can wring out of this big business."

On the contrary, there is a lot of good in the health system. So much of what is done is done right. Thus, I write this book with tremendous optimism, seeing the potential in what *can* and *should* be done.

For thousands of years, stars have been a major source of guidance for explorers—pointing the way with their light. This star serves the same purpose for those seeking to change healthcare. It is a guide, provides light, and points the way. Like for explorers finding their way, this star can do the same.

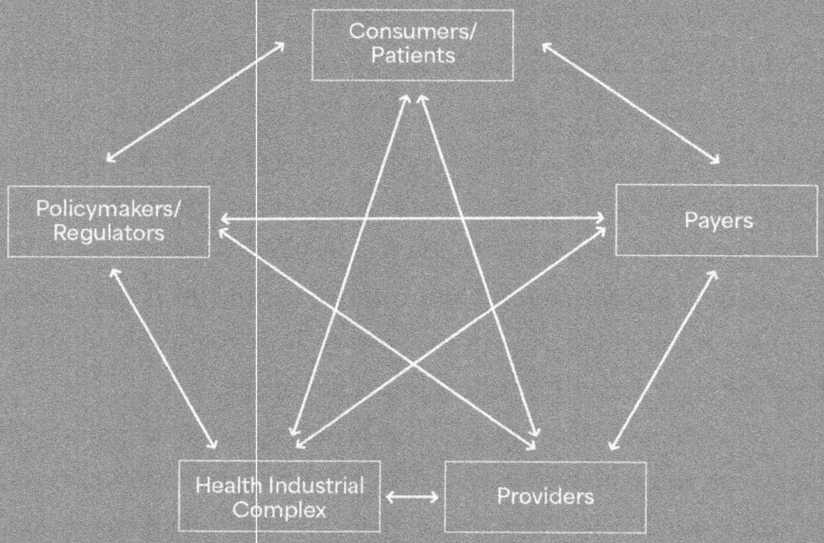
Consumers/
Patients
Policymakers/
Regulators
Payers
Health Industrial
Complex
Providers

PART 1

A Look at the US Healthcare System

The US healthcare system is the second-largest industry in this country. Serving a population of over 339 million people, the healthcare system operates across all US states. It is local, regional, and national in its focus. It is also a system of many definitions, from primary care to acute care to intensive care. These services are provided in many different locations, from clinics to hospitals to emergency and urgent care centers to private healthcare provider practices and retail stores. Healthcare is also provided over the phone and even on computers.

To provide these services, there is a wide variety of professionals in the system, including physicians and nurses, dentists, midwives, pharmacists, physical and occupational therapists, dietitians, and social workers, not to mention the large numbers of lab and radiology technicians and aides.

It is an industry that requires specialized education and licenses for practicing. It is a major financial industry with an annual spend of over $4 trillion.

Healthcare services are provided to humans of all ages. The system has grown incredibly in the past hundred years and has an influence both here in the US and elsewhere in the world through its HIC. Because of its size, it is a system that is always changing. And similar to other large major systems, there is dissatisfaction and a call to fix it.

Part 1 of this book provides two informational chapters influencing today's change initiatives. The first chapter is a contemporary look at the forces behind the overall system, including the Triple Aim; the power, control, and money in the system; the influence of the media; and the challenge of working together to make change. The second chapter is an overview of the major growth initiatives within the industry in the past hundred years, which greatly influence the healthcare system as it is today.

All of this provides a base on which to assess and plan change initiatives. To broaden our thinking, get beyond our personal perspective, and sit down at the table with others who want to create change.

CHAPTER 1

The US Healthcare System and Change

The consensus of the US population is that our healthcare system is too large, too focused on business, too confusing, too costly, and too wasteful. And because of this, for many people, the US healthcare system needs to change.

The US healthcare system is extensive and encompassing, with over $4.9 trillion in annual spending for over 339 million potential users of system services. Yet the healthcare system affects each one of us individually, as well as our families, friends, neighbors, and co-workers. It's a system that is both local and national.

Looking at the world status of the US healthcare system, one would assume that the nation with the largest GDP and economy would rank highly in terms of our population health status and our healthcare service outcomes. But in reviewing the health of our population and healthcare service outcomes in comparison with other developed countries, we don't even make the top twenty list, and sometimes not even the top thirty (Gunja et al., 2023; Reed, 2023; Schneider et al., n.d.). Clearly, there is room for improvement.

We struggle in the rankings for many reasons: diversity in population, diversity in geography, diversity in economics, and just the sheer size of our population and of our country. And we can identify examples of misses and gaps in healthcare delivery for each area. That said, we can do better, make reasonable improvements, and continue our progress. I repeat. We *can* do better, make reasonable improvements, and continue our progress.

However, while many want to change and redesign the system, before we can do this, we need to take a step back and understand both the large picture and the local one. The following four areas are significant for creating a picture of the overall healthcare system, and each of these areas is important when making changes.

The Triple Aim—A Guiding Light

In 2007, the Institute for Healthcare Improvement developed a Triple Aim framework for the overall US healthcare system, with three goals to guide it in making improvements (Berwick et al., 2008). The Triple Aim was and continues to be a major undertaking. The three goals are to

1. improve the patient experience,

2. improve the health of populations, and

3. reduce the per capita cost of healthcare.

When originally developed, these goals were worked on separately by members in the five sectors. The amazing thing is that the Triple Aim was initially seen as radical because it addressed the overall outcomes for a patient population at a time when we measured outcomes more on an individual basis. However, as we worked on making changes, the Triple Aim became mainstream, widespread, and a guiding light as we began to incorporate the three goals into change initiatives across the healthcare system sectors. In reading about each of the five sectors in parts 2 and 3 of the book, you will see the paramount issues at play in the Triple Aim framework.

Today, the Triple Aim framework sets the goals, the vision, and the driving force for the entire healthcare system, regardless of the sector. The goals are sound and sensible, and if we work together to meet them, we assume the US will improve its own health status in the country and move nearer to the top of the ranking list.

The Hidden Triple Aim—The Underside of the System

In understanding the structure and workings of making changes in the US healthcare system, we can improve the patient experience, improve the health of populations, and reduce per capita costs.

However, as an overall system, we do not work well together, which we must do to make sustainable change and achieve the Triple Aim. And not working well together has created a healthcare system perceived as too large, too focused on business, too confusing, too costly, too wasteful, and unequal in accessibility.

These are symptoms of the real problem. They are what I refer to as the "Hidden Triple Aim." How do I describe the Hidden Triple Aim? It is the *power*, *control*, and *money* in the second-largest industry in the largest economy in the world. It is competition, which results in conflicts and an inability to work together.

Let me break it down by moving around the star framework. While all five sectors seek power, control, and money, three handle the bulk of the healthcare system traffic. These three are the payers, providers, and policymakers/regulators.

Over 90 percent of the money moves through the payers sector, and we're talking about a *lot* of money. The providers sector, critical and powerful, does the actual delivery of healthcare services. Power and control are with the providers, as care is generally individually focused. Laws, regulations, and bureaucratic oversight come from the federal and state policymakers sectors executing their duty to protect the people.

While providers deliver the care and receive their money from the payers, the payers, in turn, receive large amounts of money from the government and private sources. The federal and state governments' policymaking, judicial, and bureaucratic branches provide oversight and regulatory services, and these governments pay over 45 percent of the money in the entire system to payers and providers to pay for care and run the system.

The HIC sector drives innovation and investment in science and involves a lot of money. These innovations begin with bench science and research and move to the development of products, including those used for medical diagnosis and treatment, pharmaceuticals, and biotech advances. The innovations are subsequently brought into the delivery of healthcare services through providers and, more recently, through direct sales to consumers and patients. Yet, while the impact of the work that comes from this sector in terms of new treatments is significant, the amount of money here is smaller than the money in the payers, providers, or policymakers/regulators sectors.

Finally, in the consumers/patients sector, there are over 339 million people. Control? Yes. Power? Sometimes. Money? Absolutely. This sector provides the money to run the US health system. It is money from taxpayers, employers, and individuals. And yes, while this money is used to run the overall health system that consumers and patients benefit from, it is not a direct one-for-one, and many people do not realize or think about the connections. Additionally, the consumers/patients sector is so fragmented that we often do not understand its capacity to be a significant influence. Yet from the size of major consumer and patient organizations to the power of the vote and its influence and impact on the policy sector, consumers and patients have a voice.

The Hidden Triple Aim—the competition for power, control, and money—is felt most where the big numbers lie. In healthcare, this equals the payers, the providers, and the policymakers. Yet because of the spread of power, control, and money across the healthcare system, the result is that no one sector is entirely in charge or is calling all the shots. All five sectors depend on each other. And trust me, the people working in each sector believe *they* need power, control, and money—and oh, by the way, they should be in charge.

Enter the Media

In our country, the media holds a prominent place in public discourse and in describing the US health system. The media tends to focus on issues and problems in the five sectors, bringing various perspectives that can differ based on the media outlet itself. At the same time, the media raises generalist issues that both educate the public and potentially create angst and frustration.

If we look at a summary of healthcare-related issues and concerns raised in the media, several major ones stand out. Here, I organize these headlines into hot topic areas because they are a source of more-than-average normal interest and activity by the public, elected officials, and health system leaders. You will see these hot topic areas throughout the book, affecting the five sectors:

★ **High costs:** The US spends more on healthcare per capita than any other country, yet health outcomes are not consistently better. High costs are attributed to costly medical procedures, drug prices, overtreatment, and the results of undertreatment.

★ **Administrative complexity:** Complex billing procedures involving multiple insurers, providers, and intermediaries can lead to high administrative costs and confusion for patients. Additionally, the trend among hospitals to build mega systems also creates administrative complexity and higher costs.

★ **Insufficient price transparency:** Prices for medical procedures and services are often unclear and can vary widely, making it difficult for patients to make informed decisions about their care and compare costs.

★ **Prescription drug prices:** The cost of prescription drugs is considerably higher in the US than in other countries. While this is a frequent headline, we actually spend nine cents of each healthcare dollar for pharma (CMS.gov, 2023), and considering what pharma does for the nation's health, the nine cents is a good deal.

★ **Fragmented care:** The system is criticized for lacking coordination among various providers and specialists, leading to fragmented care, duplicative treatments, and potential medical errors.

★ **Health disparities:** There are significant racial, ethnic, and socioeconomic disparities in obtaining access to quality healthcare and quality health outcomes.

★ **Insufficient preventive care focus:** A focus on acute care rather than prevention potentially leads to higher costs and poorer population health.

★ **Profit overemphasis:** Critics argue that the profit-driven nature of the system can lead to overutilization of medical services and unnecessary procedures to maximize revenue.

★ **Lobbyist influence:** There is an overinfluence by lobbyists, who serve deep-pocketed corporations, not the American public.

The media also touches on other areas, including a universal healthcare system, which is beyond the scope of this book. While it is true that other countries have universal coverage, it is a fact that in many developed countries with universal healthcare systems, many people purchase additional private health coverage to ostensibly get more and better care.

Second, the media points to a problem with employer-tied health insurance on which many Americans rely, which can lead to disruptions in coverage because of job loss or changes. In addition, there is a perception that employer-tied health insurance benefits limit individuals' freedom to choose their preferred health plan. Below the headline, however—in 2023, in the employer health benefits model, employers pay between 65 percent and 80 percent of the insurance premium, depending on various factors (including union or nonunion, single or family policies). This is still a good deal for employees.

Finally, there is a recognized bias in the media. This bias extends to its coverage of the second-largest industry in the United States. In the words of a former editor of *The Economist* magazine, journalists tend to "simplify, then exaggerate" (Mackintosh, 2023). With a system so large and complex, presenting a complete picture of any particular issue is a challenge.

Working Together and Change

When you position your thinking from the center of the star framework, you realize that no one sector outranks the others. Here, you can better see and understand the tensions between the sectors, especially between the payers, providers, and policymakers. Heightened tension exists because these three sectors are the most powerful and monied.

Talk to someone from any one of these three sectors, and you will hear what is wrong with the other two. Everyone makes judgments from the perspective of the sector where they sit, the place in the star framework from which they look at others. As the system continues to grow with the continuing development of technology and scientific progress as well as changes in the aging US population, and as the awareness of discrepancies and inequality in healthcare increases, the Hidden Triple Aim will continue threatening to derail the goals of the Triple Aim.

This is where we might be tempted to throw up our hands and dismantle the system. But the reality is that we've got ourselves a major system delivering care on an individualized basis in a country with the third-largest population in the world. We have an industry employing millions of people and costing trillions of dollars. Dismantle the healthcare system and you're begging for disaster, because the next place we might go from here will also have conflicts and issues with power, control, and money.

Nothing will change if we do not understand what we have, acknowledge the controls, acknowledge the money, and figure out how to play in the sandbox together. We need to make power a positive force. We do that by understanding the five sectors, thinking across the system, planning, and acting collaboratively with and across the sectors. We encourage people with influence to think across the system when planning and acting upon innovations. And we make the system a win–win for *all* the players involved. This is both possible and doable. To achieve it, we must do the following:

1. **Acknowledge that each of the five sectors shares the same overall goals with the others while simultaneously possessing its individual objectives.** We must keep the Triple Aim at the forefront and consider how each sector works to improve the quality, safety, and satisfaction of the patient experience.

2. **Gain a comprehensive understanding of the special interests of a sector, which invariably encompasses the Hidden Triple Aim**. This knowledge will empower us to identify and navigate highly charged and controversial items within the sector.

3. **Learn more about each sector, including our own.** We must recognize the biases, interests, connections, and perspectives. Each sector has blind spots, and we must learn what these are.

4. **Obtain credible information from legitimate sources in an effort to make sustainable changes.** Data and the information obtained from data are critical to our success in making changes. Used in creating a strategic plan, this information provides a goal to change initiatives.

Summary

For most people in the US, the very large health system needs to change. Challenges include the diversity and size of the population, geographic and economic diversity, and the size of the country. There are four areas that must be considered in planning and making changes:

1. The Triple Aim—a major national undertaking to achieve three goals:

    ★ improve the individual experience of healthcare,
    ★ improve the health of our populations, and
    ★ reduce per capita costs.

2. A set of Hidden Triple Aims—power, control, and money—which result in competition, conflicts, and the inability of the five star sectors to work together.

3. The media—an ever-present place in public discourse on the issues and problems in the nation's second-largest industry. Hot topics include

    ★ high costs of care,
    ★ administrative complexities,
    ★ lack of price transparency,
    ★ cost of prescription drugs,
    ★ fragmented care,
    ★ health disparities,
    ★ lack of preventive care,
    ★ overemphasis on profits, and
    ★ lobbyists.

4. There is an inability to work together based on the significant differences among the star sectors and a lack of understanding of how the overall system works and comes together. Yet without understanding the overall system and acknowledging the power, control, and money throughout, lasting change is not probable. Sitting down at the table together is critical in order to execute major change initiatives.

Understanding the overall system and working together using systems thinking will make sustainable and legitimate change possible. And learning from one another, as well as learning about one's own sector, is critical to success.

Only then can we make sustainable changes.

CHAPTER 2

The Star's Background

Each sector in the star framework began with a convoluted history, starting in the early 1900s. To understand the system we have today, let's get into some background that shows how, in a little over one hundred years, the US healthcare system has grown to a massive $4.9 trillion annual price tag, making it the second-largest industry in the largest economy in the world.

To do this, I will primarily focus on the twentieth century and the four significant areas of development that resulted in the growth of the five sectors that form today's healthcare system:

1. Public health (or the health of the public)

2. Modern scientific discoveries and advances

3. Private health insurance

4. Government involvement

At first blush, one might want to think of a given development area as belonging to a single sector in the star framework, but that is not the case. The development areas were and are systemwide and continue to affect how healthcare is designed and organized. Note that all these developments are designed to meet the needs of the consumers/patients sector of the star framework. Whether providing care, paying for care, policymaking oversight of the care system, or designing new treatments, the consumers/patients sector is the reason for being. Or so we might think.

Before we can make any lasting, effective changes, which is what we all believe needs to happen in one way or another, it helps to look at the healthcare system as an industry that can be changed. And here is why.

According to *Webster's Third New International Dictionary of the English Language* (Merriam-Webster, 1981, pp. 1155–1156), the definition of industry is the "systematic labor performed especially for the creation of value . . . especially one that employs a large personnel and capital; a group of . . . enterprises or organizations that have a similar structure of production and that produces or supplies . . . goods, services, or source of income."

While many people might not want to think of healthcare as a business or an industry, the reality is that money is the necessary fuel to operate the system. As designed, the system can only operate with money. Three of the five sectors (providers, payers, and the HIC) operate as businesses performing functions and services, which, in turn, are reimbursed with money. Like it or not, this is reality.

Now, let's return to the necessary background and historical developments.

Development #1: The Health of the Public

Right from its beginning, the founding US government took on the duty to protect the public. This duty is outlined in the US Constitution's fifty-two–word preamble, written in 1787, stating, "We the people of the United States, in order to form a more perfect union, establish . . . insure domestic tranquility . . . promote the general welfare . . . to ourselves" (U.S. Const. pmbl.). The key words here are "promote the general welfare . . . to ourselves."

Further, Article 1, Section 8 of the US Constitution states, "The Congress shall have power to lay and collect taxes, duties, imposts and excises, to pay for the debts and provide for the common defense and general welfare of the United States" (U.S. Const. art. 1, §8). Again, the key is to provide for the general welfare.

This way, in promoting and providing for our general welfare, a healthcare system evolved and grew over time. Here, the government assumed the responsibility of regulating a safe healthcare delivery system for all, to pay for the care of some, and, at times, to directly provide care through public (as opposed to private) healthcare delivery institutions. The government continues to fulfill this responsibility today, with mixed reviews.

At the same time, in the late 1700s and well into the 1800s, the US grew, primarily through massive immigration. Along with their talents and enthusiasm for a new world, these people brought from their countries of origin the same contagious diseases and epidemics they'd suffered at home. Add to immigration the Industrial Revolution and changes in the agricultural sector, and suddenly, we had more people living in cities in congested conditions. Here is where diseases bloomed, significantly affecting the health and safety of the population and the average lifespan.

In dealing with serious diseases, the only solution at the time was to remove the sick to keep them from spreading epidemic diseases, such as typhoid, cholera, malaria, and yellow fever, and contagious diseases, such as smallpox, measles, and others. Controlling these diseases brought about the US's first organized healthcare delivery service. In the early days, it meant trying to protect people by stopping them from contracting diseases from those who were ill.

To care for the sick and dying, religious groups and government functionaries opened almshouses—the precursors of hospitals—into which they moved the sick. Medical treatments were rudimentary and ineffectual. However, this is how organized healthcare began. As seaport cities became crowded with newcomers and transient seamen, the earliest hospitals arose in New York, Boston, Baltimore, Philadelphia, and San Francisco, among others. Government organizations began concentrating their efforts on disease control. Thus, disease control and public health protection were born.

As time moved on and modern science grew, protection of the public's health began to focus on preventing diseases before they occurred. Public health originated in England with John Snow, who showed that cholera was a waterborne disease and that, to prevent it, clean water was necessary. Disease prevention was a critical next step in public health. Once we understood our ability to alter the spread of disease, we addressed the critical need to prevent illnesses by securing safe drinking water, implementing sanitation controls, and introducing agricultural and food safety processes. These advances helped eliminate cholera, yellow fever, malaria, and typhoid in this country. This was a big win!

Development #2: Scientific Discoveries and Advances

By the late 1800s and early 1900s, the health system had grown and broadened its focus to include the treatment of diseases and conditions that had already occurred rather than simply trying to prevent them. The evolving public health perspective and medical treatments based on scientific advances spurred the growth of organized medicine and hospitals.

Soon, we saw the advancement of anesthesia and surgical procedures to treat patients. As a result, we had public health disease prevention occurring outside hospitals and medical and surgical treatments inside hospitals. These developments essentially led to the practice of medicine we know today.

Progress continued, and beginning in the 1930s, we saw science furthering disease prevention with the development of vaccines protecting the public from polio, influenza, measles, mumps, rubella, diphtheria, pertussis, and tetanus, improving the health of our nation. Add to this an array of medications, including antibiotics to treat infections, and we had a health system working to lengthen our life expectancy.

As these diseases became less common, it was no longer necessary for health department officers to be sent out to a home to post a quarantine sign on the front door notifying the public, "Stay away … measles, mumps, rubella, or fill-in-the-blank" (Rosenberg, 2020). Public health successes were institutionalized, and science continued to increase the efficacy and strength of medical treatments. As a result, public health disease protection, prevention, control, and preparedness took a back seat to a health system that turned its focus to providing care after people get sick. We saw the effects of this during the COVID-19 pandemic, when we had to scramble to reinvent concepts of disease protection, prevention, control, and preparedness for the public.

The acute care model focus appealed to the public, who reaped the benefits of treating sickness and healing from illness, lengthening the average life expectancy, and reducing infant mortality, among other health indicators. A person born in 1910 had a life expectancy of forty-six years (Arias et al., 2020). A century later, a person born in 2018 can expect to live to the ripe old age of 78.7 years (Arias et al., 2021), an almost 70 percent improvement from 1910. It is impressive.

Along with this growth in acute care, Americans adopted a different perspective on disease prevention. Our culture turned to a wait-until-illness-sets-in-then-receive-treatment modus operandi. Think about it: You see results when you are sick and then get better. When you never get sick, there are no results to see. With such an acute care focus, along with our basic assumptions of a clean and safe environment and the availability of necessary vaccines, our attention and focus on community-based public health all but disappeared.

The public focus, and thereby the American healthcare system's focus, increasingly fell on science and the ever-increasing sophistication of medicines and newfound treatments, including the ability to transplant organs, surgically repair valves, remove cancerous tissues, insert artificial joints, and prescribe pharmaceutical therapies for a wide variety of conditions. Structural social determinants of health, including food security, housing, and education, were not prioritized, because we could get more immediate results from the acute care industry and not so much from altering those social determinants.

The acute care health industry was up and running, with mission control located in the acute care hospitals. Increasingly, outpatient services, including community-based continuity of care and a primary care system, were separated from the action in the hospitals. Healthcare became progressively more expensive and inaccessible for many. And people began to need a means to pay for care.

As science and the various medical professions grew in sophistication and capability, the US overall medical and hospital industry exploded with thousands of not-for-profit and for-profit hospitals built across the US. This resulted in a significant growth in staff. Compared to other healthcare professions, nursing, with four nurses to every one of the other healthcare professions combined (Smith & Blank, 2023), grew with new educational programs and an increase in the number of nursing schools across the US. From the mid-1950s to the mid-1970s, the number of nursing programs doubled every four years (Ervin, 2017).

In addition, there was an ensuing technology build-out, including data collection and analysis for large population groups, increased bench science—including genomics and genetic medicines—and growth in academia and research foundations. Research became an industry within the larger industry. Funding was needed everywhere. Here, we see the genesis of the HIC, which is developing and conducting research for medical treatments, including diagnostics, pharmaceuticals, medical devices, and genomics research.

Development #3: Private Health Insurance

The turn to an acute care model and its ensuing costs, including large numbers of professional staff, complex treatments, specialized treatment centers, and the building of more hospitals, came with a high price tag. Billing for healthcare services became more complex with costs associated with staffing, the site of care, and numerous diagnostic tests and tools. Treatments, too, had additional costs, including laboratory tests, radiology techniques, and pharmaceuticals. Paying for all of this was no longer a matter of out-of-pocket spending.

Enter the reality of paying for care with the introduction of private health insurance in the first half of the twentieth century. There are two basic benchmarks on which the private health insurance system is built, and understanding these is very important.

BENCHMARK #1: A DEFINED POOL OF MONEY IS AT RISK

Let's start with a general definition of insurance, which provides protection against a possible eventuality. In business terms, insurance products of any type (e.g., property, fire, health, auto, and malpractice) are built with and supported by pooled monies contributed by the insureds. This money is available to pay for a significant, costly, and disruptive event for an individual or an entity that has contributed money to the pool. Everyone who contributes to the money pool is at risk of such an event or, in insurance terms, at risk for a loss. Because the future is ultimately unpredictable, we acknowledge the risk and procure insurance to protect ourselves should the loss occur. If such an event occurs, money is necessary to pay for recovery. This is money that comes out of the risk pool.

The absolute foundation of the insurance business model is the risk pools. These pooled monies are for the exclusive purpose of paying for a future high-cost/expensive loss that actuarially will not be needed by everyone contributing to the pool but will cover the costs for the person who has contributed to the pool and has a loss. The costs of such a loss are generally high, so by combining lesser amounts of money from the entire group of people who contributed to the pool of money but who will not all have a loss, when the loss happens, it can and will be paid for out of the risk pool. The idea is that many small contributions pooled together provide enough money to cover a few larger bills. This is because, while everyone in the group is at risk, the actual need can be relatively rare.

Today's private health insurance model is basically the same: a mutual arrangement with a fund that pays for the health needs of the participating population. In the private health insurance model, everyone is at risk for a serious medical incident. Everyone pools their money (called a "premium," which is combined with other premium payments in the risk pool), and when one of the participants needs to pay a medical bill, the money comes out of the pool to pay it.

If you tear your rotator cuff today, you may face a total medical bill of $25,000. The costs include diagnostic care and MRI, surgery, and recovery physical therapy. If you have private health insurance, depending on the plan, you may pay a deductible, which is paid by you and subtracted from the $25,000. The rest of the money to pay the bill comes from the risk pool. That is when you recognize that having an insurance company pay your medical bills is a terrific thing.

BENCHMARK #2: US HEALTH INSURANCE PRODUCTS WITH LARGE RISK POOLS WERE CREATED TO BENEFIT WORKERS

As the saying goes, timing is everything. As the medical profession and hospitals (the industry) launched themselves, we entered the twentieth century, and soon, world wars erupted. America's Industrial Revolution provided the means to supply and support these wars. US labor shortages followed WWI, followed by a recession. Then along came WWII, and employers introduced health insurance as a supplemental wage benefit in place of higher and more costly wages to attract and keep workers.

Health insurance was conceived as a benefit to workers and provided as a form of pay. In many ways, this is still the case. It is not a coincidence that health insurance payments are also tax-free, which is another way to reward employees without paying them more. It is a benefit because employees do not have to pay tax on the money paid for the health insurance out of their paycheck.

Early insurance companies worked with large employers. One of the first was Blue Cross, which was developed in 1929 to cover the costs of hospital services for workers who needed them. Blue Shield, created in 1939, expanded insurance coverage, paying for physician services.

Industrialist Henry J. Kaiser joined physician Sidney Garfield in the 1930s and early 1940s to cover construction worker injuries, many of which happened while building major dams in Washington and California (Kaiser Permanente, 2023). Their partnership led to the founding of Kaiser Permanente in 1945, which covered the workers and their families, providing all types of healthcare services. Private health insurance is called that because the money to pay for healthcare service insurance comes from the private businesses that put it into the risk pool on behalf of their workers. It is not comprised of tax dollars but of money from the employer's business revenue.

Along with a growing healthcare industry came associated increased costs and charges, such as hospital stays, diagnostic procedures, surgical treatments, and pharmaceuticals. The new private employer health insurance, with its risk pools used to pay for care, was necessary. The risk pools protected the workers and their families from these costs, and the increasing size of the risk pools allowed medical services and care to become more expensive.

Frankly, no one can say for sure which came first. Was it the growth of scientific discoveries and the medical industry or private insurance? It is a chicken-and-egg dilemma.

The evolution of health insurance proceeded along the same timeline as scientific discoveries and advancements, resulting in the growth of organized medicine. Add to that the US population and workforce growth and an increasing national GDP, and you have a population with more money, who can afford medical treatments and care. Before all this growth, most people could only afford to have their broken leg set if they owned an extra chicken to give to the doctor. Today, we have a population that thinks a heart transplant is fair game and should be an option for everyone.

The institutionalization of healthcare resulted in jumps in healthcare service costs. Examples included moving births from home to the hospital, providing effective emergency treatments after accidents, treating formerly untreatable medical conditions with surgery, and providing certain types of cancer treatments. This is a long way from where private health insurance coverage started. And more treatments needed more money.

Progress did not stop. The science of informatics and big data with further technological improvements came in the last decades of the twentieth century. The result was an ability to identify evidence-based practice (EBP), and private insurance embraced these developments to manage the risk pools, which, by necessity, were becoming larger and larger to cover the costs of the new models of care.

What is EBP (or evidence-based medicine)? It is a problem-solving approach utilizing scientific research to define best practices in healthcare (Melnyk et al., 2010). Created in a rigorous practice change environment, EBP is applied to patient needs and conditions to produce results that meet quality standards.

What does this mean? Using scientific research results, treatment models are designed and tested for efficacy against diseases and medical conditions occurring in patients. These treatment models meet the highest quality of care criteria, and the results are distributed to healthcare providers through professional organizations, healthcare journals, healthcare conferences, academia, and the healthcare delivery system.

In addition to assuring the quality of care delivered, EBP is intended to create consistency in effectiveness across patient outcomes. It is not a new treatment for every patient. If the treatment proposed is not supported by EBP, there are questions to be asked. This is a utilization review and is a process used by payers to review a patient's condition and the requested treatment option more closely.

If the proposed treatment does not meet EBP supported by research and peer-reviewed literature, the payer will not pay for a specific treatment and will ask for an alternative treatment option. EBP protects patients and, at the same time, helps maintain the size of the insurance risk pool by actuarially estimating the costs of care for a population. It is an important component of private health insurance.

Development #4: Government Involvement

In their first forty years, private health insurers grew to meet the working population's needs. The money in the risk pools came from the employers and eventually their employees, who, as noted, are not taxed on these premium payments. Healthcare providers and the HIC realized the risk pools were available, and the prices of their services rose. At the same time, the size of our population increased, the workforce grew more extensive, and life expectancy improved.

The federal government wanted to protect the people and make sure the healthcare industry could meet their needs, given the growth of the population. As the Constitution says, the government felt an obligation to promote and provide for the population's general welfare. This includes those people who are unemployed and do not have employer-provided health insurance, people with low incomes, and the aging population.

So enter federal government legislation and "big-time" dealmaking, with three significant congressional legislative actions over a sixty-year period, giving us the healthcare system we know today. These include the Hill–Burton Act (HB Act) (1946), the Social Security Act Amendment (1965), and the Patient Protection and Affordability Act (2010). Each piece of legislation was controversial, and each one took years to pass because of power struggles in Congress. However, negotiation and compromise were the hallmarks of reaching a consensus and passing the final bills.

THE HILL-BURTON ACT (HB ACT)

Passed in 1946 and extended until 1997, the HB Act delivered funding to build hospitals nationwide, providing facilities to care for people (Health Resources & Services Administration, n.d.). The act aligned with the growth of medical professions and the sophistication of medical practices. The original goal was to have a hospital in every town, and the money needed to build these hospitals was a combination of federal and state money. As a result, the HB Act launched decades of significant building and growth across the country, and soon, almost every good-sized town had a hospital.

The HB Act required nondiscrimination according to a patient's ability to pay and stipulated a certain amount of free uncompensated care to be provided to patients annually. However, with the continual medical inflation and high costs of hospital care, some states still had to step in and underwrite this federal HB Act requirement by providing monetary relief to hospitals to cover the costs of a portion of the uncompensated care. Private insurance did not cover everyone.

Unfortunately, in the HB Act's history, periods allowed for "separate but equal" institutions. These ended in the early 1960s with the equal rights laws terminating segregation. This was particularly the case in the Southern states, and it was not until 1967 that the HB Act's "separate but equal" discrimination clause was judicially and finally eliminated. Piggybacking on this elimination was the second major piece of legislation, the Social Security amendments creating Medicare and Medicaid.

The federal government's Medicare certification for a hospital depends on whether a hospital has an open admissions policy. In other words, there is no Medicare certification if there are no open admissions. Passing up the Medicare money flow was not a good idea.

Along with the building of these hospitals came working people and their families with insurance to cover the rising costs of medical care. The US health system was growing, growing, growing. However, a significant part of the population—nonworking people or people whose employers did not provide health insurance—was not covered by health insurance, and healthcare inflation outpaced the cost of living every year. Enter . . .

THE SOCIAL SECURITY ACT AMENDMENT

In 1965, Congress passed the second primary federal legislation, which was publicly funded healthcare payer coverage. The legislation included Medicare for seniors and people with disabilities and Medicaid for the "medically indigent." The number of patients who now had their care paid for went up exponentially. The providers sector suddenly had a large new patient population with money available for their care.

The payers sector now had two main streams of money. These included private streams from the revenue of businesses and public money from taxes. Combining these dollars spurred significant changes within the healthcare system in terms of growth and continued scientific development.

Even though eligible people in Medicare and Medicaid initially were not directly enrolled in an insurance company program, private health insurance companies grew because of their insurance business capabilities. Medicare and Medicaid contracted with private insurers to perform backroom administrative functions for hundreds of thousands of patients to keep their administrative costs low.

You might not know this, but private insurers do backroom services, such as processing provider bills for Medicare and Medicaid patients and then paying the providers using taxpayers' money from the government. In the 1990s, both Medicare and Medicaid began outright offering their coverage programs through private insurers using the insurers' money management and EBP utilization guidelines to better manage the tax payments for medical expenses.

Today, 48 percent of Medicare beneficiaries choose to enroll directly in a private insurance-managed care package, and many states use private insurers to manage all or part of their Medicaid programs (Leonard et al., 2022).

THE PATIENT PROTECTION AND AFFORDABLE CARE ACT

Initially begun in the 1990s, the Patient Protection and Affordable Care Act (ACA) was passed in 2010. The ACA created new tax incentives and health insurance offerings for people earning more than Medicaid eligibility but who did not have employer-provided health insurance. Once the act was passed in Congress and signed by the president, numerous enactments and judicial rulings followed, which included regulations concerning eligibility and the types of services paid for by health insurance for all their enrollees. These regulations aimed to broaden the reach and breadth of healthcare services for the American public.

An additional expansion under the ACA was to increase access to Medicaid. However, not all states did this. The states with higher agriculture revenue did not expand their Medicaid commitment, as opposed to the states with large industrial complex revenue, which provided state tax revenue to fund expansion.

Many of these direct-to-consumer initiatives began in late 2013 with the implementation of federal insurance exchanges and direct private health insurance sales to consumers. As part of this effort, we saw the introduction of affordable health insurance. The result was a significant reduction in uninsured consumers and patients.

The ACA also included changes in the healthcare service reimbursement model, paying for more preventive care, which broadened access to care across the system. It also required an increase in the dollar amount in the risk pools, which, as you recall, were initially designed to pay for the possible occurrence of a serious and costly healthcare incident. In some ways, the ACA was a cleanup act following the HBA and the Social Security amendments.

The ACA provides greater access to hospitals, providers, and private and public insurance than ever before. With the ACA, the number of people brought into the system with insurance coverage is impressive. Today, the uninsured rate is 8.4 percent of the overall population—a decrease from 17.8 percent when the ACA was passed (Lukens, 2023).

This change significantly impacted the number of users of the health system, the levels and intensity of care provided, and the amount of money spent. In 2020, Medicare and Medicaid comprised 21 percent of the US federal mandatory budget, and this does not include each state's contribution to Medicaid or the Children's Health Insurance Program (CHIP) (Williams et al., 2023).

In other words, out of every dollar we pay in federal tax, twenty-one cents pay for Medicare and Medicaid. This also does not include the tax dollars used to fund the national health expenditures included in the discretionary federal budget, such as the Indian Health Service, the Centers for Disease Control and Prevention (CDC), and the National Institutes of Health (NIH).

The Reality of Medical Inflation

This fourth healthcare development area brings us to the present, and we are back to the question of which came first. Which got larger first? The healthcare delivery system or the money to pay for care coming from either the private insurance risk pools created to meet the benefit needs of employees or the government tax dollars in the annual budget allocations for healthcare services?

The answer depends on how we view it. The one thing we know for sure is that medical services became increasingly expensive, and as a country, we were spending more on healthcare.

If we look back, we see that starting in the mid-1970s, the annual medical inflation rate began to outrun consumer price index inflation (US Inflation Calculator, 2024). We initially tolerated this increase because we associated this annual inflation with introducing new and better treatments for patients. So yes, the healthcare delivery system continued to grow, and with this increase in costs, there was medical cost inflation. As a result, both private and public payers needed more money to pay the bills, and they tapped their sources of money—insurance premiums or tax dollars—and continued to grow.

By the 1980s, the medical inflation rate was running over 10 percent annually (US Inflation Calculator, 2024), and the risk pools and the federal and state budget allocations needed to get bigger. Then one day, someone said, "Hold it. This medical cost inflation is crazy! We need to get this under control."

This is when the employers, who were paying for healthcare insurance for their employees, turned to the payers and demanded they address healthcare cost inflation (Porter & Olmsted Teisber, 2006). At the same time, the federal and state governments also saw a rise in medical spending, and they, too, turned to private insurance companies to manage medical costs because private insurance companies had the business know-how.

This move by the government marked the beginning of Medicare Part C, or Medicare Advantage, which gave Medicare enrollees the option of receiving their Medicare benefits through a private payer. Many state government–controlled Medicaid programs were also transitioned into the private pay sector again to take advantage of private payer medical cost-saving services.

Medical cost inflation was the beginning of managed care, case management, utilization reviews, private negotiations and contracting with providers, and provider networks. It began decades of health system initiatives to control healthcare spending. This worked, and over time, medical inflation rates fell. However, these controls initially caused disruptions and frustration among healthcare providers, consumers, and patients. It was a significant change for everyone.

Looking forward from the mid-1990s and tracking the annual medical cost inflation rate, we see a decrease. Why? Payer management practices help to reduce waste, duplication of services, unnecessary care, and inappropriate care. Is this all fixed? No, and for people who complain about high insurance costs and the burden on their wallets, there is still medical inflation, and the causes are the same in many cases.

The Healthcare System at a Crossroads

There are serious deliberations concerning the costs of care and resource allocation among the voices calling for change. Just because we can do it, does everyone deserve a heart transplant? And how do we decide who gets the transplant and who is not eligible?

In addition, we ask about the health and responsibility of the population in taking care of themselves. States have legislated guidelines for some of these questions, but they are not standard across the board and are unknown to most of the general public. These are not simply business and financial dilemmas. They are ethical concerns and return us to the reality of our healthcare model, which is to deliver care to one patient at a time. There is no single answer, and if we look back at the history and development of our healthcare system, we can point to other developments that shaped the future. It is a system of continual change.

Our modern system is designed to provide healthcare based on science and scientific progress, and that is where all these innovations have led. But we have had some serious growing pains. Our population is more than four times larger than it was at the beginning of the twentieth century. Increased life expectancy, disease prevention and control, and a safer environment are all signs of the healthcare system's success.

Once upon a time, there was money, there were health professionals and institutions, and there was government at both the federal and state levels promoting the general welfare of the population. But now, there is competition for available resources, leaving many Americans

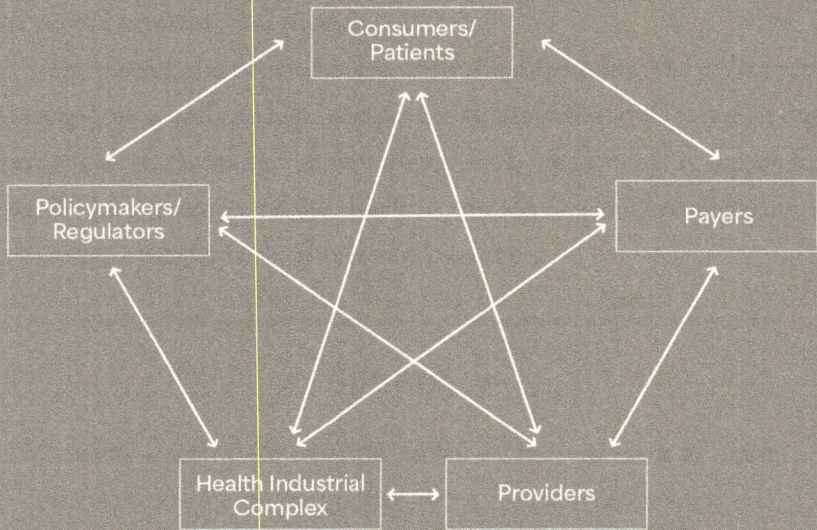

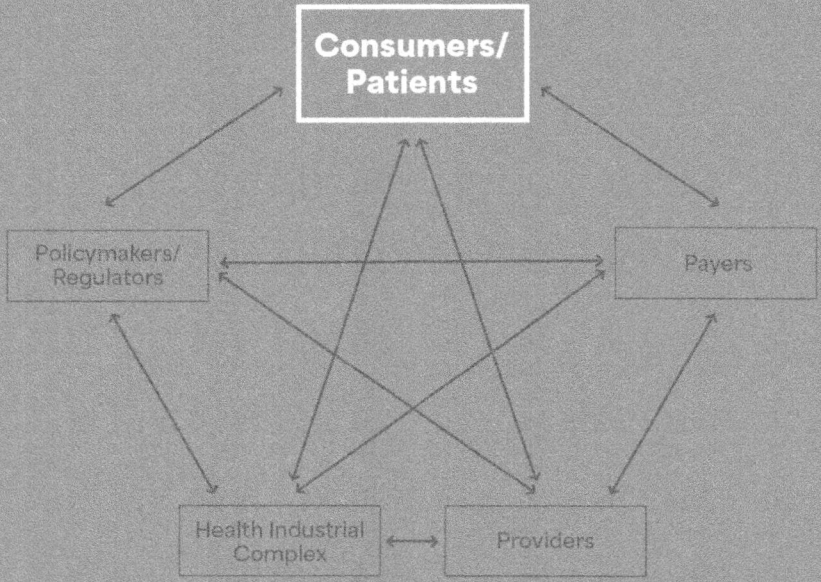

**Consumers/
Patients**

Policymakers/
Regulators

Payers

Health Industrial
Complex

Providers

CHAPTER 3
Consumers/Patients

The consumers/patients sector is the most significant. Without consumers and patients, there would be no health system. In the US, the third most populous country in the world after India and China, this sector is enormous, comprising more than 339 million people.

Changes made anywhere in the health system will affect this sector at some point down the road. Look at the arrows. All four of the other sectors connect with this sector, and there is a story to tell here.

The enormity of this sector should signal to you both the importance of the Triple Aim goals for improving the healthcare system and the opportunity for money, control, and power for the organizations and institutions involved. The bigger the player, the bigger the importance and opportunity. And this is the sector where the media's influence is greatest. The headlines go directly to this sector and have a strong effect.

Let's define the terms "consumer" versus "customer." The two words connote very different things. With the amount of money spent by many of us or on our behalf, we are the customers of the healthcare system industry. I use the term "consumer" to indicate an obligation for each one of us to participate in the system.

Participation means being involved in one's health management. Customers buy products, and whether they use them is their choice. Consumers, however, actively use the products they buy. We must use the healthcare system to get the most out of it. In other words, we must be consumers, preferably the active participatory kind.

Both consumers and patients have a powerful influence on the system. They directly or indirectly help define the necessary areas for health and scientific research and development (R&D) through their use or nonuse of the system. All 339+ million people have an effect when we look at our country's overall well-being and health. Consumers and patients also bring enthusiasm (at times), motivation (also at times), and, of course, their money to the healthcare system. It is a powerful sector.

Defining the Consumers/ Patients Sector Structure

Are you a consumer, or are you a patient? We hope that we are generally healthy consumers for most of our lives and that our status as patients is relatively short. However, through design, the healthcare system responds to consumers and patients differently, so what does that look like?

Patients are people who are acutely ill, in pain, injured, or damaged. Patients may also be chronically ill and in a medical crisis. Patients receive interventions and treatments in an acute care model with various modalities and specialties, including diagnostics, therapies, surgeries, and medications. Because they require medical services, they directly interface with the providers and payers sectors.

Consumers receive healthcare services in various disease and wellness management programs. These healthcare services are planned and not acute. Healthcare consumers also interface with the providers and payers sectors. Their relationship with the healthcare system is frequently long term, extending over years, with oversight and monitoring of their health status, as well as prevention of potential conditions or deterioration that would move them to acute care.

In the US health system, the term "patients" is used so frequently that it is difficult for many people to think of themselves as consumers rather than patients. Individually, it can be a challenge for a person using the healthcare system to think of themselves as a consumer. However, in the past few decades, there has been a turn to a consumer wellness model, which is changing our behavior and, ultimately, the system.

More health information, including health maintenance and disease prevention modalities, is available to the public. New payer models, started in the late 1980s, that pay for preventive care are influencing this shift. In addition, the development of technology and science, including genomic medicine, allows us to focus on prevention rather than waiting to apply treatments. At the same time, consumerism, or the act of "using a product," has grown significantly in our country, and we bring this way of thinking to healthcare when we take responsibility for what we want and get from the system. Think how far we have come since the early days of disease management, which included only public health protection and prevention.

Consumer health is not acute care. People with chronic conditions reside in the consumer part of the sector. When people interact with the health system as consumers, they can take advantage of preventive healthcare and wellness programs with a focus on health improvements and stable management of chronic illnesses. It is a place of active engagement in managing one's health and an area of continual development and innovation. It is also a place where healthcare cost-effectiveness can be realized.

Zeev Neuwirth's book, *Reframing Healthcare: A Roadmap for Creating Disruptive Change*, published in 2019, includes one of the best explanations of the healthcare system's customer/consumer perspective with a comparison to the patient perspective. He elaborates on the differences between patients and consumers and teases out the ethical and responsible approach of the system—a system that demands that we not solely focus on delivering overutilization, overtreatment, and unnecessary and avoidable services but also on prevention and early treatment within the guidelines of safety, quality, and cost-effectiveness.

Importantly, if we receive services as a consumer, it behooves us to behave like one by actively managing our health and our relationship with the health system. Moving away from the classification of patient to consumer is a challenge, as it also moves responsibility to the consumer to be actively involved in their wellness. Common examples of active involvement include diet, exercise, and medication management, where the consumer understands the effects of all three on their general health status and takes active responsibility to manage these to the best of their ability. Again, this is why I do not use the term "customer." Consumers actively use something they have received, and this move in our healthcare system is a critical change from the customer model.

How will a change to the consumer model perspective affect this sector? How will healthcare system leaders speak about the very real fact that consumers and patients are responsible for themselves? Will consumers and patients embrace it, or will it first need to be systematized and incorporated into the system so that there is no choice? And if we want to see change in the healthcare system, how will we design and plan changes with a consumer/patient focus? Think of the arrows between the sectors.

In reality, the US healthcare system can deliver consumer-defined services to everyone in the country through public health. We may need to remember this because our thinking is so fixed on the acute care model. Yet recall the public health response to the pandemic and our ability to dispense COVID-19 testing, vaccines, masks, and changes in public schools and transportation systems, to name a few. Because our healthcare system is designed and executed on a one-person-at-a-time basis, we don't think of services provided to large groups.

Let's look at the 2020 pandemic, which forced the increased use of telemedicine and virtual care and a more defined allocation of services. For the most part, we see that patients and consumers have embraced these new models, with their convenience and efficiency being important benefits. The new world of making an appointment for wellness management at a grocery store pharmacy, Zooming with our primary care provider for a checkup, or using Cologuard versus a colonoscopy for routine screening is a significant change for everyone. Consumer healthcare is growing and will continue to do so. Decreasing medical costs and bringing more people into the system at a less acute level of care are the critical outcomes of this consumer model.

For others, patient-as-victim can be a preferred status, not just for the patient but also from the provider's perspective. We see it frequently. Yet each person is ultimately responsible for themself, and the acceptance of new service modalities, such as telehealth, retail store clinic sites, and wristwatch monitoring, is telling us something.

Lifestyle choices are up to the individual. The consumer mindset means adopting a new way to make decisions regarding diet, exercise, use of medications (prescribed or unprescribed), self-care, preventive care, and care responsibilities for others who cannot manage themselves. And while motivation is a key factor here, so are knowledge, awareness, and understanding of what one needs to do and how to do it.

It would be best to only give someone a wrist monitor for cardiac arrhythmia after clearly explaining what it is for, how to use it, and what to do with the information gained from the readouts. It is a consumer/patient/provider relationship and depends on mutual respect and trust. This execution relationship is another factor to include when planning and designing change.

How Many People Use the Healthcare System?

You might not realize this, but out of the over 339 million people in the US, we do not know precisely how many people use the healthcare system each year, either as consumers or patients. This includes not knowing the number of patients actively receiving treatments and the number of consumers who are participating and are well. Yet these factors can help us plan changes when looking at the whole population.

Through population health initiatives and research, we do know the untapped needs of the population to some extent, and we can estimate our capacity to provide services to all in one way or another—not necessarily the high-tech care we often think of as healthcare but certainly public health protection and prevention services. Our provider organizations exist for major catastrophic events, so if large numbers of consumers/patients undergo a health or medical catastrophe, there is a level of treatment available to meet the incalculable need. Remember this term: "a level of treatment."

In an attempt to solve the mystery of how many people use the health system each year, the federal government has made efforts to introduce a universal patient identifier, similar to the social security number, which could conceivably count the number of individuals using health services. However, privacy concerns have blocked the adoption of this effort, and progress has yet to be made (VanHouten & Brandt, 2021).

Therefore, we estimate. One way to do this is to look at the number of people who have access to healthcare services through a source of payment. According to a Kaiser Family Foundation (KFF) report from 2022, 55 percent of the total US population had private insurance either through their employer (48.7 percent) or non-group coverage (6.3 percent), 21.2 percent of the population were below the federal poverty line and had Medicaid, 14.6 percent had Medicare, and 1.3 percent had access through military programs (KFF, 2022). In a subsequent study, approximately 7.7 percent of the population were uninsured (KFF, 2022; Peterson-KFF Health System Tracker, 2024).

However, there are often fluctuations in these percentages, as we observed during the pandemic. Economic variations can alter the mix of these percentages, especially when job losses result in people also losing their employer health insurance coverage. Still, looking at the source-of-payment numbers is one way to estimate how many people can access and use the system in a consumer or patient model of care. It helps in planning and allocating services aligned with the state of the population, as well as the provider's capacity.

New Relationships with Healthcare Providers

When proposing new programs and frameworks for care models, we see that consumers and patients are now exploring new roles and relationships with healthcare professionals (HCPs). On an individual basis, consumers and patients want to work collaboratively with their providers to achieve and maintain a state of wellness. They view their providers as expert guides who assist them in maximizing their health.

The wide range of healthcare providers specializing in various areas, including mental health, nutrition, and physical therapy, offers many options for treating long-term chronic illnesses. This type of long-term relationship, a departure from acute care, requires both the consumer/patient and the provider to operate differently. These new models include continuous care, follow-up, self-care, and provider case management.

With telemedicine and virtual healthcare in an increasingly electronic society, many consumers and patients have indicated that they favor these options and access to various providers who work in these electronic settings. Because of the inconvenience of leaving work and traveling some distance, it is easier to schedule a telemedicine visit with a social worker or dietitian rather than an office visit.

Behavioral health services have also significantly expanded with the introduction of telemedicine, and the impacts on rural healthcare have been significant. These services complement the medical model based in the examining room. Therefore, as we think about change in the consumers/patients sector, we should consider these relationship options, including the use of other specialty support areas as part of the intended improvements.

This is not to take away responsibility for maintaining a healthy lifestyle, which is best accepted solely by consumers/patients. Cardiovascular disease remains the largest killer of people in this country. The leading drivers of heart attacks and strokes are tobacco use, hypertension, and air pollution, all of which are preventable (Frieden, 2022). It is critical that consumers and patients take ownership of their health, no matter their status.

Patient Advocates and Special Interest Groups

Anybody who watches, listens to, or reads the news is familiar with consumer/patient special interest groups that influence outcomes in the healthcare industry. These influential groups include the American Cancer Society, the American Diabetes Association, and the American Heart Association. There are hundreds of them.

Remember that this is the second-largest industry in the US, and the consumers/patients sector is the largest of the health system's five sectors, so everything associated with this sector is significant. When making changes, these consumer/patient special interest groups can be helpful, or they can be hindrances to an initiative. These groups have been in place for years, and they address the interests of consumers and patients in various ways. There are also groups that provide legal advice at no cost, especially when a consumer/patient is involved with a payer dispute.

These special interest groups can be local and small or national, large, and powerful. They can be wealthy and use their money to support research and new treatment options, to lobby policymakers, and, in some cases, to pay for care. Some groups direct their attention one-to-one, such as La Leche League, where moms support new moms in breastfeeding and caring for a new infant. Other groups call attention to and support research and treatment for orphan diseases, rare diseases that affect fewer than 220,000 people in the US (Haendel et al., 2020), or common diseases that have been ignored because they are much more prevalent in developing countries than in the US.

For the most part, when the focus is on meeting the needs of consumers and patients, special interest groups can be valuable for individuals and the healthcare system in general. These groups are committed and focused, and they call attention to the issues and needs of specific populations.

The power of this sector can also translate into the power of the vote. A national nonprofit consumer/patient organization with an operating budget of millions of dollars, which represents the interests of hundreds of thousands of members who vote, has a great deal of influence.

Make no mistake, these organizations spend money and lobby at the federal and state levels. In 2021, lobbyists spent $356.6 million (Investopedia Team, n.d.) representing healthcare issues related to consumers, patients, and businesses. These included pharmaceuticals, medical products, and nutritional and dietary supplements. Yes, the intention behind these efforts is to benefit consumers and patients. However, these lobbying endeavors can have a significant influence across all five healthcare sectors. Think about the arrows.

Major Issues in the Consumers/ Patients Sector

In chapter 1, we highlighted the goals of the Triple Aim. Here, we discuss the issues around the Triple Aim in the consumers/patients sector, including

- ★ access to care,
- ★ safe care,
- ★ cost-effective care, and
- ★ unnecessary care.

To understand and manage these issues, it's vital to think from the center of the star. We like to believe that healthcare system leaders should consider consumers and patients when planning to make changes in the healthcare system; however, consumers and patients often seem secondary to the planner's goal—especially when we are told, "Now, this is the way things will work," without much consideration for our needs and wants. Nevertheless, consumer/patient issues strongly influence innovation processes, new and efficient service adoption, and sustainable success. They can also make or break the changes.

Consumers/Patients Paying to Support the System

When asked about this, consumers and patients often respond that healthcare costs too much and that those who use the services pay too much. The media and the individual relationships within the system constantly remind us of this. When planning a change from the center of the star, consider its value proposition and the burden of high costs for consumers and patients. This is an ongoing and never-ending problem and conflict. The impact of the costs of care and services must be discussed in every change conversation.

Think about it. Consumers/patients are the primary source of the $4.9+ trillion that runs the system. How so? We pay directly into the system when we pay our insurance premiums, putting money in the risk pools that are used to cover healthcare services.

We directly self-pay for deductibles and coinsurance. We pay for uncovered services. We consumers/patients pay our taxes that are used to support almost half of the annual medical spending in this country. We indirectly pay when the prices we pay for retail goods and services include the costs incurred by manufacturers/producers to provide their employees with health insurance benefits. The consumers/patients sector supports it all (Keehan et al., 2023).

Just to break it down, in 2022, roughly $471 billion of the $4.5 trillion annual healthcare spending (CMS.gov, 2023d)—10 percent— was paid directly by consumers/patients. This leaves $4 trillion paid through the payers sector, which comprises private and government payers, including charities and special interest groups. And $471 billion is a significant out-of-pocket payment factor for consumers/patients.

The out-of-pocket issues here are individuals' healthcare costs, whether they use health services or not. If you have private insurance, you send money—your health insurance premium—to the risk pool to ensure that should there be an unexpected medical emergency, there is a means to pay for it. You may never need money from the risk pool, but you have paid into it.

Besides paying health insurance premiums, taxpayers support government-funded healthcare programs through federal and state income taxes. These programs include Medicare, Medicaid, and CHIP. It doesn't matter that you have also paid a premium into the risk pool for your health insurance coverage. You still pay taxes.

If you use healthcare system services, you may accept these payments. For people who do not require acute care, even with preventive and wellness services added to the list of essential services in the 2010 passage of the ACA, most think they spend too much money. When asked, they complain about high costs—costs that include insurance premiums, deductibles, co-pays, and coinsurance.

Of course, there are differences in how and what consumers/ patients pay for care. Their mindsets differ too. One may say, "I am paying too much." Another might say, "Wow! I didn't pay anything for that!"

Some will pay their premiums, satisfy their patient responsibilities (co-pays and deductibles as necessary), take advantage of some preventive/maintenance services, and pay their taxes. Without any major health needs, they have little else to think about regarding such needs. Others shop around for healthcare and look for a provider who is right for their medical or financial needs.

Some pay an additional premium directly to the provider for "concierge" status. Some people are willing to pay anything to get better, while others believe healthcare is a right and that they should pay nothing. Some have no choice but to take what they can get in an underserved area, which can be right in the middle of a large city or far away from any town.

Let's return to the issue of want versus need and say you want a hip replacement. After reviewing your case, your insurance company applies an evidence-based treatment recommendation, which indicates that the hip replacement is unnecessary and that you don't need one. This is an all-too-common want-versus-need situation and is frustrating for patients and providers alike.

In *The Long Fix*, Vivian Lee (2020) writes that many experts believe that up to 30 percent of the money spent on healthcare services is wasted because of overtreatment, duplicative treatments, and inconsistent practices. This is $1 trillion. Lee and other experts think consumers and patients must understand what waste means.

In the book's chapter titled "A Revolution of Common Sense," Lee notes that once consumers/patients accept the reality of waste and over-treatment, they will better understand their role in waste, overtreatment, or duplicative treatment cases. Experts suggest that to fully understand this, consumers and patients should ask questions about their proposed treatments and the costs involved and explore all treatment options. If the answer needs to be clarified, ask again and again.

This brings us to the subject of medical debt, a topic directly related to paying to support the system. Studies show the burden of medical debt, as seen in two reports issued in 2022: one by the

Consumer Financial Protection Bureau (CFPB, 2022) and the other by the Urban Institute (Karpman et al., 2022). The CFPB dashboard contains information derived in February 2022 from a nationally representative panel of de-identified, consumer-level records from a major credit bureau. Here, medical debt is the most prevalent type of debt in collection and shows up on people's credit reports.

The CFPB research shows $88 billion in medical debt on consumer credit records as of June 2021 (CFPB, 2022, March 1). Using the CFPB data, the Urban Institute reports the median medical debt as $707. The percentage of people who have medical debt and do not have health insurance is 9 percent. The average household income for this group is $92,324 (Karpman et al., 2022).[1]

Putting aside who pays what, might people be avoiding health-care services in the first place in order to prevent or avoid increasing medical debt? In a Commonwealth Fund (2023, October 26) survey, many Americans, regardless of whether they had health insurance or not, noted that they delayed or had forgone healthcare due to already significant medical debt. The result was a worsening of their health problems. If this is happening, they are missing wellness management, which could prevent higher cost care farther down the road.

This sector is the target audience of the media. Headlines that include high-cost issues, prescription drug costs, lack of price transparency, health disparities, and lack of a preventive care focus are targeted to this sector. Is the media accurate? Only sometimes.

Yes, there are individual cases and situations where these headlines are accurate. And yes, many of these issues have been or are being addressed with a national response. This is a large industry, and par-

---

1   If someone is eligible based on low income and within federal poverty limits, Medicaid picks up the cost of healthcare. Therefore, this population is not included in these study results.

ticipation on the part of all to make corrections takes time. Sometimes, it takes years. Using a healthcare example—unlike the emergency room, where things happen immediately, many headline issues are like chronic illnesses. They are treated over a long period and with the participation of many.

Summary

Over 339 million people live in the United States, and all are entitled to healthcare services. The consumers/patients sector is by far the largest of the five sectors. Traditionally, this sector has been viewed as one in which individuals are expected to use healthcare system services at some point.

However, times are changing, and we are experiencing new models of care focused on self-responsibility and population health outcomes. Do not forget that this sector is the source of the money used to run the healthcare system, whether through direct payments for health insurance coverage and its associated costs, providing tax dollars to support government health benefit programs, or purchasing retail products where a part of the product cost covers the employer's employee health insurance benefits.

In this chapter, there are four essential areas to understand:

1. The US health system serves consumers and patients with a different care model for each group:

    ★   Consumer healthcare can be long term and include chronic illness management and general health maintenance.

★ Patients are people who are acutely ill, in pain, perhaps in a medical crisis, or damaged. They may require intense care and significant use of health system services.

2. Healthcare services have expanded into different venues based on the wants and needs of consumers/patients:

★ With the growth in the population, there has been increased access to a wider variety of providers, including mental health, social services, physical and occupational therapy, and nutritionists.

★ Telemedicine and expanding access to providers in nontraditional healthcare sites, including pharmacies, have increased the healthcare system's ability to meet healthcare convenience needs.

3. Consumer/patient advocacy groups number in the thousands and are generally connected to a special interest on behalf of their membership. They provide research funds, lobby policymakers in both state and federal locations, and offer consumer/patient support. They can be powerful and influential.

4. The Triple Aim goals reside in this sector. Quality of care and safety must be a top priority as population health initiatives for large groups gain attention. Medical debt is a concern and may prevent consumers/patients from using the system.

A population of 339+ million is significant, making this a big sector. Without consumers/patients, there is no health system. Monitoring and serving the general population's needs are critical.

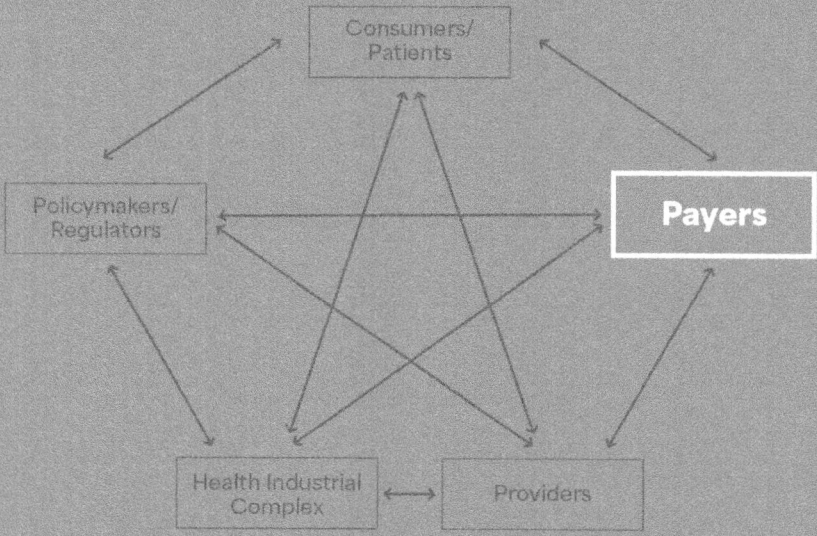

Consumers/
Patients

Policymakers/
Regulators

Payers

Health Industrial
Complex

Providers

CHAPTER 4

Payers

When talking about making changes to the US healthcare system, many consumers, patients, providers, politicians, and media personalities target the payers sector.

Change ideas in the payers sector run from the extreme of the total elimination of payers to the taking over of the payers sector by another sector. At the same time, the payers sector is not a part of many system change efforts, and many people, both within and outside the healthcare system, have yet to learn how this sector works. As a result, when planning changes, payers tend to be ignored rather than brought into the conversation.

As you can imagine, this causes a problem because it can become a question of the sustainability of change as time goes on. Change what you will, but at some point, someone will invariably ask, "Wait a minute, who is going to pay for this?" Let's not forget that the healthcare system is an industry, money is the fuel that runs it, and payers are the primary source of that money.

Let me begin this chapter with three caveats. First, if you are not from the payers sector, you don't know what you don't know. I say this based on extensive experience in the system seated at the star's center.

You need to know a *lot* about payers because this is a complex sector. If you don't know much about this sector and do not factor in payers in the planning process for making changes, initiatives are likely to fade before they make it to the boardroom table.

Second, when it comes to the Triple Aim, payers are fully on board. No one gets up in the morning with the intention of providing less-than-quality healthcare services (Triple Aim #1) and not aiming for cost-effectiveness (Triple Aim #3). Unlike the other sectors, payers have the unique ability to see from a population perspective because of the large numbers of covered lives—the lives they are responsible to pay for (Triple Aim #2). In other words, payers are a source of important information. While consumers/patients can experience this sector individually, the payer's work is to see and pay attention to trends, not only individual people.

Third, the Hidden Triple Aim is indeed at play here. This sector draws cries for change, and change initiatives usually address issues related to power, control, and money. Get payers, providers, and policymakers into a boxing ring, and you'll see them slug it out, even as each turns to the audience and proclaims their right to be the victor.

With these three caveats in mind, let's move to the star's center to see how this sector is constructed and how it works.

Defining the Payers Sector

To begin, I will state the obvious: The purpose of the payers sector is to provide money to pay for healthcare services.

To get a handle on its size, we know that after retail, the US healthcare system is the second-largest industry in our country, and it is growing. US national healthcare spending is predicted to continue increasing by 5.7 percent annually because of an aging population and overall population growth. The Centers for Medicare & Medicaid Services (CMS) actuary office predicts that we will spend $6.8 trillion annually by 2028, which will be 20 percent of the GDP (CMS. gov, 2022; Poisal et al., 2022). This projection was made before the pandemic, which may alter those figures.

Going back a few years to 2019, based on $4 trillion annually for US national health expenditures, private and public health insurance programs paid 75 percent of people's healthcare expenses. Third-party payers and public health paid 10 percent; other sources, including direct payments from charitable organizations, researchers, and grants, paid 10.5 percent; and consumers and patients paid 5 percent (Advisory Board, 2020). Excluding the 5 percent, or $200 billion, paid directly by consumers and patients, $3.8 trillion passed through the private and public payers sector, which is the money we refer to as people's benefits, whether the money comes from private or public sources.

Since the money that runs the health system comes from the private and public payers sector, they typically wear the bull's eye. Until people need money, like our friend with the torn rotator cuff, this is typically the sector that everyone is angry with for many different reasons. Making a change in this sector will be felt across the star.

The Source of the Money

As already stated, the payers sector is powerful and big. With $3.8 trillion going through the payers, whether the source of the money is private funds or government revenue, our attention needs to be here.

Where does the money come from? There are two primary sources. The first is premium dollars paid into private insurance risk pools by employers, employees, individuals, and unions, among others. The second is public insurance programs. Yes, in many ways, Medicare, Medicaid, and CHIP are public forms of insurance or assurance, run by the US Department of Health and Human Services (HHS) and paid for by taxpayers through federal and state taxes.

We use the term "insurance" here, as it is an assurance that the government will pay for the cost of care. As I noted, taxpayers are frequently the employers, employees, and individuals who are paying twice into the healthcare service payment buckets—in the form of private insurance premiums and tax dollars.

There are significant differences between these two money sources. Private insurance premiums are paid directly into the insurance company's risk pool, where they are managed and invested to keep the pool full. Insurance companies in this country are highly controlled and overseen by state regulators. The regulators review the risk pool investment models, and if the costs of care are higher than anticipated, meaning that a private insurance company needs to increase the amount of money in the risk pool by increasing premiums, it must get approval from state regulators before it can do so.

Some large employers are self-insured, which means they keep the premium money in their own risk pool and pay for healthcare costs using the insurance company as an administrative services organization (ASO). The ASO conducts backroom services, including accounting, determining and paying benefits, and preparing government reports, among other business functions.

Should the healthcare costs run high and threaten the self-insured employer's risk pool, these employers and their employees and insureds are protected from the higher-than-anticipated healthcare costs by a required stop-loss insurance policy. Such a policy picks up the excessive charges and pays (stops) the losses from the self-insured's risk pool. No matter the private risk pool model—insurance company or self-insured employer—it is regulated by the government to protect the employees and insureds throughout.

By contrast, public insurance or assurance programs are mandated by law. Such extensive programs as Medicare, Medicaid, and the Children's Health Insurance Program (CHIP) have a fixed funding mandate as part of the federal and state budgets. There is no risk pool. Medical spending is estimated and is a budgeted line item.

These health assurance programs do not have discretionary spending, and if the costs of care for public program patients are higher than anticipated, money is available either through an increase in taxes, a shift of tax dollars from other programs, or a deficit recorded in the government debt. The government can do that, while private insurance cannot.

Interestingly, the mandatory budget does not include all health programs, and Congress makes allocations to fund these discretionary programs. The Indian Health Service, the CDC, and the National Institutes of Health (NIH) are included. Veterans' healthcare has both mandatory and discretionary components. The ongoing debate concerning the national debt and mandatory spending rears its head in this universe (Cubanski et al., 2023).

A Business Culture

This brings our attention to the fact that no matter the source, the payers sector operates in a business culture. This means it can be competitive but is not inflexible, and it has proven willing to innovate and change over time.

Remember the business responsibility for the private payer risk pools. These risk pools need to be managed to keep them liquid and sufficiently funded to pay for care costs. Payers need money to operate. Like every business, there must be a profit to be viable. Such labels as "for profit" and "not for profit" are related to tax status, and every entity, whether classified as for profit or not for profit, must make enough money and be profitable to exist.

Many people who want to change the healthcare system point to the business culture as an indicator of why payers need to be eliminated from the healthcare system, which itself is a human right. They believe that the business culture and human rights are not like-minded and that the business culture's profit mentality is at the heart of the problems associated with high costs and consumers' and patients' inadequate access to a source of payment for care.

However, the payers' business culture is only partially responsible for the high costs of care and inadequate access. In response to their customers, the employers, and the federal and state governments, the payers have stretched and innovated for decades to control costs and improve access. Because of the size and interrelatedness of the sectors, it would be easier to redesign the healthcare system with the payers. And don't forget, the private payers pay taxes too.

If we look at how a private insurance company's premium dollar is allocated, applying the 2012 ACA medical loss ratio (MLR) requirement, we find that 80 to 85 cents go to paying for healthcare services and quality improvement, 10 cents for administration, and 5–10 cents for taxes and profit (CMS.gov, 2023c; Insurance Matters to CT, 2021).

Most people associate business with money, and throughout this book, I point out the significantly large money numbers in our system. But do not forget that the delivery of healthcare is a people-run service industry. It involves labor-intensive work, with staff who need paychecks, money to purchase supplies and equipment, and money to build and maintain facilities. It all costs money to get the job done.

If you turn to our trusty star's arrows, you will see the flow between the two sectors on the right, both of which include a financial component: the payer and provider businesses. From this perspective, money is the fuel that runs the system. We cannot get the job done without it.

Like all the sectors, the payers sector is driven by a recognized need to reduce the rising costs of healthcare and improve access to care. This is a Triple Aim item. In business terms, this means maintaining and growing the customer base, working closely with one's customers to meet their needs, paying for quality and safe healthcare services, and working with the other sectors to systematize the operations for effectiveness and efficiency. In a healthcare system this size, it is truly a challenge.

Say what you want, but the US healthcare system would fall apart without payers. Providers often duke it out in the ring with payers, but they still need them. An essential business model component is the contract between the provider and the payer.

I believe this only seriously began in the 1980s, but it is now the norm for providers and payers to negotiate and contract healthcare services. When consumers/patients want to receive these services, they must be sure that the provider accepts payments from their specific payer. The acceptance of a specific payer payment is one of the reasons why you must show a card indicating who the payer is for your services when you go to an appointment and check in. If the provider does not have a contract with your payer, you either must pay out of pocket or find another provider who accepts your payer. This inconvenience is an area of incredible frustration for consumers/patients.

There are major control and power plays here at the contracting table, with providers on one side and payers on the other. At times, it hardly seems that consumers and patients are a priority.

Who are the biggest payers in this sector? Like everything else, this has a complex answer. Looking at the overall dollar amounts, the government pays the most. Based on a 2023 CMS report, the federal, state, and local governments account for 50.6 percent of the money spent. Private funds from employers and households account for 42.8 percent. Private revenues, including research monies, charitable dollars, and individual payers, account for 6.5 percent (CMS. gov, 2023d).

However, in managed care, which is a model designed to reduce waste and pay for the proper care at the right time, the government sources a portion of the 50.6 percent contributed via tax money. It runs the money through private payers as administrators, as they have the expertise to manage the payment for the care provided. In other words, the government says, "You can do this better than we can, so take the money and spend it efficiently." And the private payers do it better.

The five largest private payers are UnitedHealth Group, Elevance (Anthem), Centene, Kaiser Permanente, and Humana. Each provides managed healthcare services and insurance-type benefits for private customers and some public programs, such as the Medicare and Medicaid models. These sizable private payer corporations, alongside the government, have led efforts to control costs by introducing innovative care-based payment models to the overall healthcare system.

These innovations include managed care, value-based payments—where bonuses are paid for specific outcomes in patient care services—and payment-based models that bundle payments and prospective pay.

Their commitment to the Triple Aim is demonstrated in their change efforts, which affect everyone across the star system.

Unfortunately, once the ACA required its medical loss ratio model (MLR), the payers acted to maintain profits by setting up business mergers with pharmacy benefit managers (PBMs), healthcare provider organizations, and retail and specialty pharmacies. When the companies in these vertically integrated relationships with the payers billed the insurers for their services, a portion of the billing organization's profits flowed back to the payers in a less-than-transparent model.

The overall responses to the MLR requirements were industry consolidations, reduced competition, and increased costs. A pharmacy benefit management (PBM) owned by an insurance company could raise its prices for the insurer, whereby a portion of the money ultimately made it back to the insurer (Walker, 2023).

Who Is the Customer?

Payers have agreements with a wide variety of entities. The first tier is insurance purchasers, including employers, unions, and individual insurance buyers. These customers, the insureds, provide the funds for the risk pools that the payers manage, and they benefit from the risk pools when the need occurs.

Payers have a second customer tier, which is there to meet the needs of the first-tier customers and get paid for their services out of the risk pool. This second tier includes healthcare providers, provider networks, and PBMs. Using the Medicare fee schedule as the base, reimbursement fee agreements are negotiated and contracted between payers and the second-tier customers, providers, or provider representatives referred to as provider networks.

The first-tier entities benefit from these contracts. When negotiations between the payers and the second tier become contentious, you may see this in the press as a disagreement between a large payer and some providers as they work on a contract for the payer's insureds to be eligible for treatment at a specific treatment center by the center's providers. It never looks good to the public. Never.

Payers Are Not the Enemy

What does private health insurance do besides manage the risk pools? And how do they control expenditures? In my insurance role at a Fortune 100 company, we followed the Triple Aim and paid a fair price for healthcare services that met quality standards, were cost-effective, and worked to assure patient satisfaction. Because of our size and national model, we did impact population health. This is an example of the opportunity in front of the payers.

Our team of leadership professionals was critical to ensure quality and effectiveness. The team included healthcare providers (nurses, physicians, and therapists), underwriters and actuaries, customer service, attorneys, claim payers, technicians, and operations specialists. This combination of people worked to ensure that healthcare was delivered to patients through qualified medical providers across the US. In addition, since each state has unique healthcare regulations, we needed these leaders to ensure that we met the individual state requirements.

We had four goals driving our strategic and operational planning. First, we systematized operations to assure quality through consistency of healthcare services provided by contracted healthcare providers across the US. During this time, there was a significant growth in information technology, and medical researchers in large numbers used health and biomedicine information to develop evidence-based guidelines and practices (EBP) for diagnosis and treatment. Using these EBP guidelines, health insurers like us became important vehicles to assure safe and quality care.

We worked with providers to meet quality and safety requirements using evidence-based guideline software as the standard for case management and utilization decision-making and to assure consistency across our national operations. We received national accreditation from the Utilization Review Accreditation Commission (www.urac.org) to assure consistency and act as a benchmark for well-trained and managed operations. Not all providers were accepting of this, and case management and utilization reviews continue to be hot-button items for some providers and, in turn, their patients.

This is when a provider states, "The insurance company made me do this," or "The insurance company won't let me do this." Instead of remaining silent, maybe we, the patients, should say, "Why won't they? What are their reasons? Are there research-based alternatives to my treatment plan?"

Second, we took responsibility for the timely and correct payment of medical bills. Insurance companies use a turnaround time measurement, which means the number of days from the receipt of an accurate and complete bill for services to when the money is sent to the provider. Payers set realistic payment goals, which are met through large billing centers located across the country. In our company, if the care provided was evidence-based medicine and authorized (if necessary),[2] the bills were paid on a timely schedule. The providers did not have to wait for payment.

In terms of payment amounts, medical bill reimbursement rates are negotiated with the provider networks, bringing stability to

---

2   Most care does not require insurance company authorization.

provider payments. Oftentimes, pharmacy discounts are also obtained through a PBM to stabilize the payment process, backing into the risk pools and, ultimately, the premiums. Yes, these large provider and pharmacy networks charge a fee for their services, but the money paid out allows for standardization and performance criteria and can assure the quality of care.

Our third goal of payer responsibility was to protect patients from fraud and malpractice as appropriate. The role of insurance companies is to authorize and pay providers in good standing, with medical licenses and healthcare accreditations. Unfortunately, despite public opinion, there are people providing healthcare whose licenses have been suspended or revoked.

The worst I encountered was a chain of clinics set up in an urban site with unlicensed "providers" giving healthcare advice while seated around a folding table—there was no patient exam room—who submitted medical bills under a single provider ID. And yes, fraud goes both ways. There were patient claims made for accidents that never happened. Clinics ordered durable medical equipment that was never delivered to the patients and ended up elsewhere. It was eye-opening and showed the realities of a healthcare system designed to serve more than 339 million people.

The fourth goal was to act as an ASO. Federal and state public programs and large self-insured employers/entities—which means the employer keeps and manages its own risk pool—pay private insurance companies to do this oversight work *for* them. This work is referred to as backroom work, and insurance companies are paid a fee by the government or a self-insured entity for these services.

Insurance coverage often crosses state lines because of the size and scope of an employer's business and its health insurance benefits for its employees, as well as the nationally focused federal assurance programs. Both self-insured employers and governments need services to manage this scope, which is another reason why another sector cannot simply take over as payers.

The key word is "simply" because, while there are well-known payer/provider companies like Kaiser and Geisinger that do excellent work, it is complex. These payer/provider organizations have similar incentives for both the payer and the provider and are more likely to minimize total losses. And yes, consumers/patients benefit here. It is technically a win/win/win model.

When I worked in a national payer leadership role, I traveled extensively to our regional offices and was amazed at the differences in treatment models across the US. These differences are influenced by local provider perspectives and focus. Because of the treatment differences and state regulations, I often said, "If you've seen one state, you've seen one state."

The Price on the Bill

Something that may surprise you is that different payers pay different prices for the same treatment. Take our friend with the rotator cuff injury. Providers (or their networks) negotiate with payers and contract with a payer to determine how much will be charged by the provider and paid by the payer for a service. Providers generally accept payments from several payers, and because of these unique payer–provider contracts, every payer pays a different amount for the same service. So when billing the payer for the rotator cuff repair, the provider's bill reads according to the negotiated rate for that specific payer.

These negotiated charges and reimbursements are based on the Medicare base rate. Medicare established this rate, and it has been controversial since it was implemented over 30 years ago. Including the

American Medical Association's Resource-Based Relative Value System Update Committee and the Medicare Payment Advisory Committee (an independent legislative branch agency), there are many and varied voices that provide input and respond to the Medicare base rate. Medicare makes the final decision; however, it can be contentious, as seen in the past decade, with reductions in payment rates to providers. There is plenty of coverage of this in the press.

The Medicare base rate is used to negotiate payment rates between private payers and providers, which are all different. Regarding our rotator cuff injury example, a private insurance payer's payment amount is different from Medicaid's or Medicare's for the same injury and the same treatment mode. For private insurance, the agreed-on fees charged by a provider and the payments made by the payer are a percentage of the Medicare rate. The fees charged by providers are often 120–150 percent or more of the Medicare base rate, which is the extra money that the providers claim is necessary to offset their losses from Medicare and Medicaid. This is because, when the payer is Medicaid, the provider receives less than the Medicare base rate for the same service.

The backstory is that providers are not getting paid the same thing. If they take Medicaid patients (and some provider organizations, particularly public and not-for-profit hospitals, are required to do so), Medicaid is the payer of last resort, meaning it pays providers the lowest amount, which is less than the Medicare base rate. And oftentimes, providers say they cannot deliver care at the Medicare base price, much less the Medicaid base price (American Medical Association, 2023).[3]

---

3   Note that hospitals cannot refuse treatment to anyone regardless of their ability to pay. When they provide care for patients whose care is paid for by the lowest payers and patients whose care is paid for by the highest payers, the highest payers make up the losses from the lowest payers' payments.

Thus, providers transfer this loss of money or shift the costs to private insurers, known as the cost shift, to make up the difference. This means that when my company contracted with providers, we paid a fee for healthcare services that was a higher percentage of the Medicare base rate. We had no choice if we wanted to ensure that our insureds could receive treatment from this group of providers.

All these contracts that establish payment rates between payers and providers were considered the proprietary business information of both the payers and the providers and were unavailable to the general public. But providers are businesses, and in 2021, the federal government passed the *No Surprises Act*, requiring them to list their price schedules. The providers met this requirement with resistance. The same act also contained rules concerning the surprise billing of patients with no health insurance coverage or patients who receive care from a provider that is not in a provider network contracted with the patient's payer.

This continues to be worked out. In addition, beginning in 2022, payers have been required to report what they pay to providers on behalf of Medicare beneficiaries. Here, there is also resistance that remains to be worked out (CMS.gov, 2023, September 6; 2024, March 15).

Another view of the cost shift model is that if private insurance pays more than the government to cover the monetary losses that the providers say are incurred in government business, then the private insurers are spending more from the risk pool. They may have to increase their premiums to pay these higher costs. However, state insurance commissioners must approve such private insurance premium increases, and they know that the state-funded Medicaid program is the payer of last resort and the lowest payer.

I assume the commissioners understand the need to increase private insurance's finances by raising premiums to cover the cost shift; thus, they approve the premium increase requests. In Connecticut, for instance, the press reports these negotiations. However, I have never seen a single mention of the cost shift. The higher costs of care billed to the private insurers result in a turn to the insureds to add to the risk pool money with higher premiums and to reduce the drain on the risk pool by paying higher deductibles and co-pays to the providers. These increases can be significant and are a primary source of complaint. Overall, these actions have resulted in incredible frustration.

Payers, both private and public, see the healthcare system across a broad scope. While there is power, control, and, of course, money involved, these basics are part of what drives the Hidden Triple Aim and lands these sectors in the boxing ring.

Summary

The payers sector is complex. In a healthcare system the size of ours in the US, a significant amount of money resides here, resulting in power and control struggles. Ultimately, the money comes out of the consumers' and patients' pockets, resulting in the payers sector being a target of the media and a place where discussions concerning healthcare often begin. Yet the payers sector is too frequently misunderstood by the other four sectors and is unfortunately left out of conversations concerning creating change. Not fully understanding this sector is a challenge for the health system.

In this chapter, there are four primary areas to understand:

1. The two major types of payers and their funding sources are the following:

   ★ Government program payers, including Medicare, Medicaid, CHIP, the Department of Veterans Affairs (VA), the CDC, and the NIH, are funded by employee/employer payroll taxes, Medicare premiums, and federal and state tax revenues.

   ★ Private insurance payers maintain risk pools funded by insurance premiums from employers, unions, employees, and individuals. Health insurers may also receive government money in payment for administering managed care plans for Medicare (Medicare Part C or Medicare Advantage) and Medicaid programs. They may also administer self-insured plans for large employers and perform backroom services for government and other large plans.

2. Payments to providers encompass the following:

   ★ Government programs pay providers, such as hospitals, professional networks, licensed professionals, and pharmacies, the Medicare scheduled fees and the (lower) Medicaid fees.

   ★ Private insurance payers pay fee rates that they negotiate with provider groups using Medicare rates as a starting point.

3. As for cost shifts, providers negotiate with private insurance payers to contract fee rates that are higher than the Medicare rates to offset their losses on Medicare and Medicaid payments, which do not cover their costs. These charged fees often run between 120 percent and

150 percent of the Medicare base rate. Insurance payers must set premiums that are sufficient to cover the higher payments, and the premiums are subject to regulation by state insurance commissions that recognize the necessity for covering the losses from lower-paying sources.

4. Payer/provider organizations such as Kaiser and Geisinger have demonstrated success. Creating a model that brings together two major sectors, payers and providers, has benefited consumers and patients.

5. Payers are key to the success of the Triple Aim goals. In their payment relationships with providers, payers have every incentive to achieve

   ★ quality and patient satisfaction to ensure efficient, effective, and safe treatment;

   ★ population health improvement by expanding access to and coverage for health services; and

   ★ cost-effectiveness to eliminate unnecessary, costly, or ineffective treatments and prevent waste, fraud, and abuse.

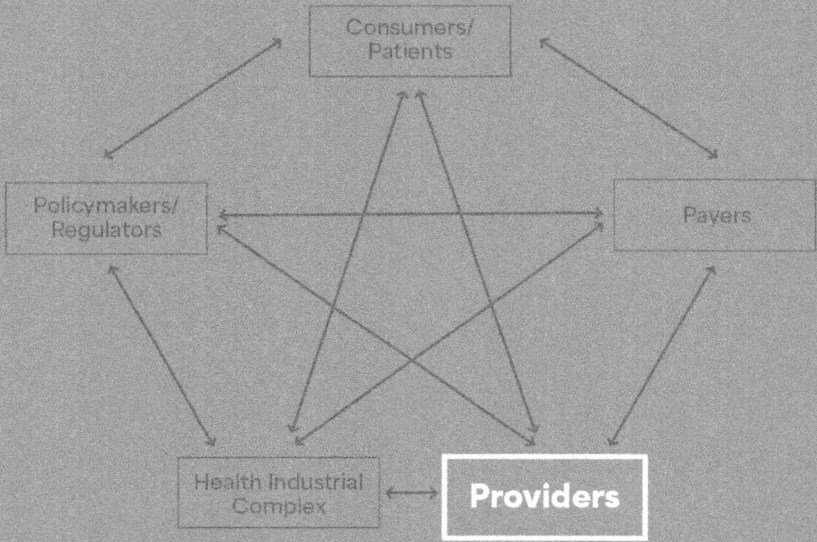

CHAPTER 5

Providers

In the past forty years, the private sector has changed dramatically in delivering healthcare. Gone are the days when the private practitioner physician saw patients in the office, admitted them to the local community hospital, made rounds in the morning and afternoon to write orders for hospital staff, and was on call for telephone inquiries 24/7.

The role of the physician provider has changed, and the community stand-alone hospital providing inpatient-only services has too. The providers sector is now a world of big and sometimes multistate corporations with large numbers of employees working in direct patient care and support services. These services include laboratories, diagnostics, home care, rehab, informatics, financial services, billing centers, and purchasing departments.

When you look at this arm of the star, you see two major parts: the individual health care professionals (HCPs) providing healthcare services and the healthcare facilities providing the sites for delivering healthcare services. Here, everybody is providing.

Most of the trillions of healthcare dollars are spent each year in the providers sector. In this sector, dollars are *revenue*, translating into *expenses* in three sectors: payers, the government, and consumers/patients. The providers sector comprises various large and influential segments: a large workforce, large corporate entities, small facilities, and specialized care facilities, all located throughout the US.

The providers sector is where medical care takes place—where consumers, patients, and providers come together. It's where diagnosing, treating, and healing occur. Medical care is called "care" for a reason. It is a source of what helps people and can improve their lives.

The providers sector is a major influence on costs and access to care, the two areas that bother people most about the US health system. This is the site for the greatest Triple Aim opportunity and, when seen in its entirety, the sector with the greatest complexity. It, too, is oftentimes the origin of the Hidden Triple Aim. Think about the complexity, the size, and the amount of money and shake your head. It is almost overwhelming.

If we want to see change, we need to understand this sector and start by looking closer at the professionals in the examining room who deliver healthcare services. But remember, healthcare services are no longer just delivered in a doctor's office or hospitals, clinics, long-term care facilities, and, yes, in homes. Now, healthcare is delivered in local big-box retail or pharmacy and grocery stores and through virtual telehealth visits. People working in these various sites provide care based on the stage of patient acuity at the time they see the patient. And this acuity defines the types of care in this wide variety of locations. No matter the site, providers must be licensed and follow their specific professional practice guidelines.

US Healthcare Professionals by the Numbers

The healthcare industry, a people-run service industry, has grown significantly in the past fifty years and will continue to grow as the population ages and the HIC introduces new technology, continues to grow the genomics industry, and enhances therapeutics. This growth calls for more professionals to provide the increasingly sophisticated services delivered in institutions. At the same time, we need to get clear on matching the professional categories with acute and less acute conditions. Some professionals specifically provide these varying levels of care. To create change, it is essential to understand and manage this reality.

I will use the term "HCPs" to refer to physicians, nurses, and therapists. When necessary, I will differentiate between HCPs based on their education, training, licensure, and specialty areas.

Based on 2022 data, roughly 7.3 million licensed HCPs in the US are working with consumers and patients. When we look at their education and training, these 7.3 million represent a highly educated workforce, which, as you will read, influences the costs of care and access (Smith & Blank, 2023). All 7.3 million are required to have a license to care for consumers/patients, and, in some cases, additional certifications related to specialty practice areas are necessary.

Additionally, there are another 7.4 million healthcare workers, including personal care aides, nursing assistants, medical and dental assistants, and various technicians who are trained in a specialty area but not required to be licensed. Notably, many healthcare system change suggestions come from these frontline providers, and their voices need to be heard and addressed. Think about them when you stand at the center of the star.

LICENSED PROVIDERS

Nurses, includes registered nurses (RNs), advanced practice registered nurses (APRNs)/midwives, licensed practical nurses (LPNs), DNPs, and PhDs: 4.2 million

Physicians, dentists and osteopaths, and physician assistants: 1.3 million

Physical therapists (PTs), occupational therapists (OTs), respiratory therapists (RTs), psychologists, and nutritionists: 1.4 million

Pharmacists: 375,000

As a people-run service industry, HCPs are part of a big business with much power and control. As such, HCPs sometimes do not readily welcome change in the healthcare system, especially when their expertise is challenged and their ability to run this moneymaking sector is affected. This is true for changes introduced from both within and outside the sector.

Many HCPs believe they are so well educated and trained that no one outside the providers sector can understand the complexities of healthcare delivery. Even within the providers sector, as the number of degrees and status climbs, a culture erects barriers and sometimes blocks innovation. Everyone in every sector supports this culture, including the policymakers in licensing and accreditation, the payers who pay providers more according to the letters after their names, and the consumers and patients, who for the most part believe that "doctor knows best" and want the best and brightest to get rid of the pain, particularly when they're hurting. As for the HIC, they have figured out that if you can make money benefiting the providers, they will get on board and support new initiatives.

Make no mistake, money influences this sector, as does control and power. They cannot be separated. This sector is home to influential advocacy groups, including the American Medical Association and the American Hospital Association. These are two of the many groups that work throughout the star sectors and hold great power and control, influencing the direction of change. They are a source of information, and their status can be helpful in the change-making environment. However, they can also block change-making efforts.

Education, Training, and Work

With an increased demand for sophisticated care, major changes in professional education requirements have added more years of learning and training to the various professional groups. With an education and training hierarchy (look at the letters at the end of a person's name), the more education and training a person has, the higher their organizational status rises, accompanied by the expectation of a return on investment in power, control, and money. The standard for paying for care is that the more highly trained the staff is, the more one should and can be charged for the care provided. Paying more for more highly qualified HCPs is generally accepted, not just in the provider sector but across the entire star.

For decades, physicians, dentists, and psychologists had doctoral degree requirements. Now, professional doctorates are required for pharmacy and for physical and occupational therapies. With its multiple practice levels and large numbers, nursing has national goals for both a bachelor's degree and doctoral preparation.

As healthcare providers have become better trained and the HIC has delivered more sophisticated treatment tools, we've grown more accustomed to seeing them help save the formerly untreatable. Expectations for patient care outcome improvements have expanded for all. This includes consumers, patients, and healthcare providers.

We've created an endless loop in which more complicated medical procedures require more learning and training and increased associated costs in facilities. The higher those costs, the more revenue for the healthcare providers, treatment facilities, and research centers. Miracles do occur, but so do major disappointments, and sometimes, the reality of a patient's situation seems a harsh wake-up call when, in fact, it is precisely the reality.

It is essential to recognize the work involved in providing healthcare services. Ideally, it is teamwork. Working bedside is a 24/7 job and is physically demanding, as well as mental and emotional work. Assessment skills and critical thinking are absolute necessities, and every person—yes, every person—at the bedside is assessing and evaluating according to their training and education. This applies across the HCP spectrum, from the medical assistant to the most lettered and educated specialist.

While healthcare services outside of the bedside setting may seem less intense, critical thinking and assessment skills are required and can be even more vital in getting the best care at the right time and place. In general, we would like to have consumers/patients in the bed only if necessary, and other care should take place in a less intense setting.

The Models of Care

Moving from the individual HCP delivering healthcare to consumers and patients, we look at the various models of care. These include trends in the delivery of services, as well as sites of care and their organizational structures. Much of this has occurred in the past seventy-five years and relates to both the changes in the payment models and the building of hospitals, clinics, and treatment centers across the nation.

PRIMARY CARE

While we often think of hospitals when talking about the delivery of healthcare, most healthcare services are delivered *outside* of hospitals. Outside of hospitals, the models of primary and chronic care are designed to meet the needs of consumers and patients.

What is primary care? It is care designed to provide basic services to support and maintain patients' health (Collins Higgins et al., 2015). This is where accountable care organizations (ACOs) and medical home models are located. An ACO is a treatment model with a financial component.

The Centers for Medicare and Medicaid Services (CMS) developed this innovation model for Medicare with the goal of coordinated care, ensuring patients get the right care at the right time, avoiding unnecessary duplication, and preventing errors (CMS.gov, 2024, January 29). The number of ACOs continues to grow, and this is important because ACOs have been shown to have superior quality performance compared to similar physician groups not participating in an ACO. Moreover, ACOs have generated year-over-year savings for the Medicare trust fund.

"Medical home" is another term that describes a primary care model organization that coordinates comprehensive care, is patient-centered, incorporates community-based services, provides 24/7 access to an HCP, and meets quality and safety standards. It includes a team of physicians, advanced practice nurses, physician assistants, nurses, pharmacists, nutritionists, social workers, patient educators, and care coordinators (Agency for Healthcare Research and Quality, 2022).

This wide variety of professionals provide primary and chronic care and are the professionals we may see over a lifetime. With the present-day predominance of specialist physicians who tend to work in hospitals, the professionals in these two models are important and valuable. The medical home is a twenty-first–century model, and there are ACOs and medical home models throughout the country.

Clinicians in these models are accountable for the quality of care and healthcare costs and must meet quality benchmarks and spending targets. These models impact patient satisfaction, improve functional health status, and decrease emergency room use and hospital readmissions. For example, you may receive care from a professional in an ACO or medical home model and not even be aware that it is the model. You would say, "I just had an appointment at the doctor's office."

HOSPITALS AND HOSPITAL ENTERPRISES

Hospitals deliver a model of acute care with specialist physicians and other practitioners. With 31 percent of the total annual medical spending on hospital expenditures, let's take a close look (CMS.gov, n.d.-b).

In 2022, there were more than six thousand hospitals of all classifications in the US (American Hospital Association, 2024). The category list includes large, small, pediatric, psychiatric, veterans, not for profit, for profit, public, private, urban, and rural. Some have university affiliations, and some are associated with religious faith organizations. Others are known as critical access hospitals and others are part of the Indian Health Service. Like the patient type classifications, these are just a few of the many healthcare provider institution categories we have today.

As already discussed, our first hospitals emerged in the late 1700s and early 1800s. Like everything else in healthcare, they have changed. The hospital-based enterprise concept has grown significantly, and many hospitals (though not all) are now part of large multisite and sometimes multistate provider systems. These enterprises include traditional hospitals, outpatient facilities, surgery centers, urgent care centers, physician practices, diagnostics, and labs.

Hospitals employ HCPs. The most obvious are nurses. According to the Bureau of Labor Statistics, 70 percent of the nursing workforce works in hospitals (U.S. Bureau of Labor Statistics, 2020). As of 2022, 74 percent of physicians working in various sites are employed by hospitals (Physicians Advocacy Institute, 2022). This shift was largely due to the pandemic (Gooch, 2022).

These enterprises, with their large workforces, serve millions of people and hold significant power, control, and money. Their primary purpose is to empower the individual entities in their enterprise system to deal with the health payer system and conduct business in a competitive environment. Do not think there is no competition for patients. On the contrary, look at the advertising on billboards, newspapers, and magazines, to name a few, and the positioning of certain specialties, such as orthopedics, cardiac services, and cancer centers, to attract patients. The hospital industry is very competitive, and not only do they compete for patients, but they also go after big-name professionals, insurance contracts (yes, even those), and academic affiliations. Sometimes, they believe they are the center of the health system universe.

The most prominent organization in accrediting health care sites is the Joint Commission, which provides accreditations that must be renewed every three years. The original commission has been in place since the 1950s. The Joint Commission grew in response and established a significant national footprint in the 1960s when the federal government mandated that Medicare and Medicaid pay the hospitals that were required to have Joint Commission accreditation. As the appendix of this book provides, there is much more to learn about hospital accreditation, provider certifications, and sources.

The top five healthcare provider enterprises are HCA Healthcare, Veterans Administration, Common Spirit, Ascension Health, and LifePoint Health. In 2023, these five enterprises included 20 percent of US hospitals (Behm et al., 2023; Healthgrades for Professionals, 2023). In addition to serving large geographic areas and large numbers of consumers/patients, these hospital systems are powerful in the federal and state policy arenas. As businesses, they resist transparency pricing and consider their contractual agreements proprietary to their businesses. The influential American Hospital Association resides here and is a multimillion-dollar-per-year advocacy and lobbying group for the trillion-dollar hospital industry.

Trust me, when we look at the negotiating table between providers and payers in these power settings, it is pure business, with the relationship contractually defined. It can get ugly if a contract expires before reaching a new contract agreement. Without a contract, these provider systems regard patients insured by a payer as out of the provider system's network, resulting in higher costs for the patient and even denying patients access to their HCPs.

This is a business that plays hardball. We often hear of this from the payer viewpoint, where the provider is a "non-participating provider." However, when the shoe is on the other foot, the hospital or physician practice declares that the payer is a "non-participating payer." In both cases, the patient pays the costs. These contracts are between the healthcare delivery systems and the payers, and while the patients wait for the outcome of the agreement, they tread water in the risk pool to which they have contributed. This is frustrating, to say the least.

With the increasing size and growth of hospital and professional systems, antitrust suits have begun, including a large suit financed by a private philanthropist targeting three major US systems. In addition to locking in providers and threatening access, these large systems promised to reduce the costs of care, which has yet to happen (Evans, 2022; Gonzalez & Becker's Hospital Review, 2022, June 13).

Smaller community and rural hospitals are also essential. They may need more significant funding, but they are significant in terms of serving the population. According to the American Hospital Association's Fast Facts from 2020, 30 percent of US hospitals are in rural areas (American Hospital Association, 2024). This brings us to the next rallying cry driving change in the healthcare system: access to care. Here, we refer to access as having a place to receive care and a means to pay for it.

Look at any map of the US, and you will see large rural areas where people live and, like the rest of our population, require healthcare services. This group of the population is often underserved, leaving them with a major access-to-care problem. The formation of critical access hospitals, first designated through the federal Balanced Budget Act of 1997, was an attempt at a solution to this need.

These critical access hospitals have the criteria of being located more than thirty-five miles from another hospital, providing access to emergency care 24/7, having twenty-five inpatient beds or fewer, and having an average length of stay of less than ninety-six hours for acute care. Moreover, of course, there are medical cost issues here as well. To maintain financial stability, many of these hospitals have organized into regional partnerships (Hostetter et al., 2023; RHIhub,

2023). Others have formed relationships with large medical centers in urban areas, providing a referral option.

Aligned with a partnership or not, the National Rural Health Association, a nonprofit nonpartisan membership organization serving rural communities including rural hospitals and clinics, cites various issues that contribute to health inequities and disparities in low-population areas. The issues include workforce shortages and a problem delivering mental health services, exacerbated by lower availability of mental health professionals and even acceptance by the population of the need for mental healthcare. Telehealth has undoubtedly helped with this, and the VA system is an excellent example of telehealth services for veterans living far away from a site of care. Nevertheless, access to care remains a big problem.

Socioeconomic factors, such as higher percentages of poverty and lower average incomes, also affect rural America's healthcare. These factors are worse for minority communities and children. There are also higher incidences of chronic illness, as well as a greater frequency of injured people and fatal crashes (NRHA, n.d.). The rural population is a challenging one with challenging needs, contributing to the low overall rankings for US healthcare and impacting our ability to meet the needs of over 339 million people.

Another change in place relates to fewer solo physicians and dentist practitioners working in our communities. Now, there are large provider corporations unaffiliated with a specific hospital. These corporations have their own outpatient services, such as diagnostics, labs, and treatment centers. And yes, the amount of money moving through the healthcare system has attracted investors. While these provider corporations were originally set up as independent corporations, they are being bought up by insurers and private equity investors, which are now where the vast majority of physician practices reside.

These private equity enterprises are for profit and are moving large amounts of money throughout the enterprises. In some cases, this has caused severe problems for hospitals. The problem begins on the investor side, where payouts can be high. On the provider side, if there is a lack of funds, this can impact the ability to pay the costs associated with direct patient care, including staff salaries, and can jeopardize patient safety.

While some states have tried to oversee private equity investments in healthcare, in December 2023 a US Senate bipartisan committee began an investigation into the impact of private equity ownership of hospitals (Grassley, 2023; United States Senate Committee on the Budget, 2023). At the state level, there are also investigations into the safety and ability to provide and manage hospitalized patients (Evans & Weil, 2024).

Again, business, business, business. Many of us have a difficult time associating business practices with the delivery of healthcare services. Until the private equity controversies related to hospital bankruptcies and the descriptions of these business models and the impact on patient care delivery were covered by the media, most people were unaware of the profit-making perspective of healthcare entities. (Abelson, 2023; American Hospital Association, 2023b).

A positive business model includes such provider/payer organizations as Kaiser Permanente and Geisinger. These organizations are structured to bring together both providers and payers into a single corporation, which aligns the incentives of both sectors. Their demonstrated success relates both to care of consumers/patients and financial interests. And this is accomplished by minimizing total losses versus at the cost to one or the other.

Moving Away from Traditional Healthcare System Models

Community-based care is designed to meet consumers and patients in various settings. It is reaching millions and bypassing the "hospital as the center of the universe" model. It factors in social determinants, including the income status of consumers and patients, and operates in many locales, including large city neighborhoods and small towns. The first to create innovative healthcare delivery models, the HIC partly drives community-based care.

Thanks to initiatives begun in the early 2000s, we now have pharmacies, grocery stores, and large retail stores offering healthcare services (Burkle, 2011). Healthcare is available at convenient care clinics in stores such as CVS, Rite Aid, and Publix grocery stores, to name a few. The staff in these convenient care clinics are fully licensed and accredited HCPs, including nurse practitioners, physician assistants, pharmacists, and physicians. They are well organized and follow evidence-based guidelines for diagnosis and treatment. Ownership by major corporations ensures that the practices meet healthcare regulations and standards, and state regulations dictate the practitioners' scope of practice.

At first, these large retailers got into this service because they had a pharmacy with a licensed HCP who provided a component of healthcare treatment, including instructions on medication use, side effects, and contraindications. They were delivering healthcare. Retail clinics have been well received because of their convenience and effectiveness in treating basic illnesses and administering medications and vaccines, including for influenza and for COVID-19 during the pandemic.

Generally, they are open seven days a week, with evening hours to accommodate working people. More access sites have resulted in a drop in hospital emergency room visits, where treatment has been costly and often unnecessary. They have also created a major shake-up of the legacy healthcare system. If we add telehealth to these multi-channel access sites, significant changes will be seen ahead—all to be discussed, refined, and maximized with systems thinking from the center of the star.

An example of this successful model is CVS Health Corporation, which is a company spread across the US that provides both in-store and home delivery services. Some stores offer basic and urgent care services. The services include telemedicine and expanded home infusion, where patients receive IV medications right in their homes, thus avoiding a trip to the clinic.

These retailers who set up outpatient clinics in their stores already had a large customer base coming and going every day. They could afford the investment necessary to set up a clinic that met the regulatory requirements and hire licensed healthcare providers who understood and complied with evidence-based primary care treatment models.

This business model has come a long way since CVS opened its first Minute Clinic in 2000.[4] We now have CVS's purchase of Aetna insurance, which has again changed the scene because it's a provider owning a major national payer. Aetna's national health insurance and Medicare Advantage program customers have access to the CVS array without being referred by another provider. This convenience is good for consumers.

And here it seems like the tail is wagging the dog. Another of the two sectors, a provider and a payer, have come together to create and deliver new models of care.

---

4   CVS originally stood for Consumer Value Store.

The move away from traditional healthcare delivery models has come a long way. Zeev Neuwirth (2019) describes it as reframing healthcare, reorienting our thinking, redesigning, and reorganizing.

What Gets in the Way of Cost Reduction and Access?

Currently, only 29.9 percent of physicians and 43 percent of nurse practitioners work in a primary care setting. Yet primary care is where we find most consumers and patients (Antono et al., 2021; HRSA, 2023). Among the physicians practicing in primary care, only 39 percent are family physicians (AAFP, 2015).

For the other 70 percent of physicians not practicing in primary care, the attention to specialist training goes along with an acute care model. More surgery, more acute care treatment models, and more technology in the diagnostic and treatment phases require further training. If a physician begins training after graduating from medical school, works in a sophisticated medical center with research models, and goes to school to continue training, they will ultimately want to use their training in practice regularly. The major reason physicians with specialist status stay away from primary care after all their training is that they work in hospital systems, preferably in large cities, where they can perform cutting-edge work.

While we point to this lack of primary care as a reflection of the strength of the acute care model, it is an access-to-care problem in cities and rural areas and affects population health, which is part of the Triple Aim. The increasing frustration of the overall population regarding getting an appointment with a physician can be addressed by promoting medical homes and ACO professional teams. People, including the providers themselves, need to continue working within the framework of these new models.

Let's face it: *Acute* care is more costly than *primary* care. The high-tech interventions practiced in big hospitals are a big cost for the system. As mentioned previously, in her book *The Long Fix* (2020), Vivian Lee details the causes of high costs within the system and notes that 30 percent of the money spent on healthcare—about $1 trillion— is unnecessary. Lee writes that the money goes to pay for waste and fraud, unnecessary overtreatment, and new treatments that are too expensive and not automatically more effective. The basic cause? A high-tech industry, the acute care mentality, and a patient population that frequently expects immediate results with, at times, little accountability for their health lifestyle. There is a place for efficiency, which is lacking as of now (Lee, 2020).

High-tech interventions occupy far more space on the treatment options menu than the primary care health management variety. Think about it. It doesn't take a lot of degrees and specialized training to work with consumers and patients to adjust their diets, manage medication protocols, take on therapeutic physical exercise programs, and introduce accommodations into a home to factor in a change in ambulation. Yet our societal attention on advanced education degrees and certifications drives the perspective of acute care interventions/treatments.

Currently, there are 155 medical schools in the US (International Medical Aid, 2023) and forty-one osteopathic medical schools (American Association of Colleges of Osteopathic Medicine, n.d.). Osteopathic medicine delivers a more holistic, whole-person model of care and has the same licensing, prescribing, and treating practices as MDs.

Acute care interventions can sometimes be too much, yet acute care is frequently—some might say too frequently—considered the standard of care.

Billing: Where You Really See the Costs

To better understand the costs and possible excess, let's take a step back and look inside the providers sector at how the billing system works. It's mighty interesting.

Traditionally, providers billed using a fee-for-service model, calculating and charging for every item and treatment separately. For hospitals, where 31 percent of the overall money flows, a hospital-specific chargemaster is managed by the hospital's finance department, with specific charges on the bill for treatments, procedures, supplies, pharmaceuticals, and room rates, among other items (RevCycleIntelligence, n.d.).

Are the charges the same as the actual costs, determined by calculating workforce time, supplies, and facility expenses? No, the charges are not the actual costs and are often more than the actual costs. Recall the cost shift description in the payers sector. The cost shift is a change in the costs of care from one payer to another, which shows up on the bill as different charges for the same item on the bill of another payer, depending on the contracted agreement.

Providers control the cost shifts. To cover the care costs for every patient, the provider shifts the costs of care from a payer source, which pays less than the actual costs, to a payer, generally a private insurance company, which pays a larger amount. These are the contractual agreements between the provider and the payer. To secure a contract with a provider and list the provider as a participating provider in the insurance company's list, a private payer will agree to pay the provider more than the base rate cost.

Control? Indeed, the participating provider, rather than being the underdog in these arrangements, is controlling the scene. "Pay us what we want, and we will participate in your plan. Don't pay us what we want, and you can tell your insureds they will have to go somewhere else for their care." This is the Hidden Triple Aim, big time!

So the charge appearing on the bill is subject to adjustments based on the contractual agreements between the provider and the payer, not the costs to deliver the care. Note that if a patient does not have a third-party payer, which is what we call self-pay, they are responsible for the charged amount, which can be very expensive. Discounts are infrequent. Chargemaster operations are so vital to the hospital billing process that they are considered a specialty in many hospital administration master's degree programs.

Billing for every treatment and procedure individually and being paid for each item is one reason for skyrocketing costs. However, we know from the payers sector that attempts have been made to change this individual itemized (or fee-for-service) billing. Some of these initiatives include payment structures, such as bundled payments, prospective pay, managed care, and capitation, which use the charges associated with the contract. All of this interfaces with the chargemaster process. While there have been some improvements in reducing care costs using these payment structures, this is an ongoing challenge.

For institutions such as hospitals, outpatient clinics and treatment centers, diagnostic centers, rehab, long-term care, hospices, and home care agencies to bill, they must be licensed and approved. Many of these institution bills include a bill from the individual provider, who also must be licensed and have a national provider identifier (NPI) listed on the bill. An individual provider can be a physician, nurse practitioner, certified midwife, physician assistant, or mental health provider.

Here is a source of controversy: submitting a bill using the NPI of a provider who did not see the patient but provided oversight. For example, a bill uses a physician's NPI with a higher reimbursement rate (recall the status of the letters after one's name) rather than the NPI of a nurse practitioner or physician's assistant. This billing practice is referred to as "incident to billing" and is allowed by some payers but not others. Hidden Triple Aim is stamped all over this issue.

A payer mix adds a further twist to the bill and is a composite listing of all payers paying a provider. (Recall that I described that for a single treatment, there are a variety of payment amounts made to the providers, depending on the payer agreement.) Using the Medicare fee as a basis, which is established based on the costs of the treatment, payers may pay more or less than the Medicare fee.

For example, if a treatment costs $100 and the Medicare fee is set at that rate, the payer is billed based on this amount, which is adjusted according to the contract between the payer and the provider. If the payer is Medicare, the provider will bill Medicare and be reimbursed $100. If the payer is Medicaid, the provider may be reimbursed only $60 for the same treatment. If the payer is a private insurance company, according to the contracted rate, the provider will bill more than $100 based on the contract with the payer, which, for example, is 150 percent of the Medicare base rate, or $150.

Providers need to balance out this mix of reimbursements, analyze their payment sources, and make certain they are not operating at a loss. This is referred to as the payer mix, and it is an important function of the financial office.

I have seen examples of this not working, including a clinic opened in San Francisco to treat people experiencing homelessness. After operating for three years at a loss, the clinic closed because there were no other patients with payers who paid more to compensate for the losses of treating uninsured or even Medicaid-covered patients. Specific outpatient clinics, such as federally qualified health centers established to provide care to the underserved, have their reimbursements protected by a designation from HHS, and they do not operate at a loss.

Getting Paid

Producing a bill and submitting it to a payer sounds simplistic. For many bills, this continues to be the case. However, prospective pay, bundled pay, and value-based payments have more complex billing requirements. Additionally, the application of reimbursements within an organization is complex. Prospective pay includes both outpatient and inpatient care, diagnostics, and sometimes home care as well. Applying the money across a multitude of departments is complex.

Value-based payments introduced by the federal government and followed by private payers have also changed the financial scene. Bonuses and penalties for specific patient outcomes add a new dimension to the revenue stream. These outcomes are measured at the bedside and directly result from patient care. It is another link to the provider organization's duty.

As we've already covered, private equity has entered the providers sector, with investments being made in physician organizations and large hospital systems. Additionally, private equity dollars are invested in research and technologies that can provide digital offerings to limit costs, improve quality, and expand access to care. These private equity dollars are a bet on financial success and reflect the big dollars associated with specific patient care organizations.

Summary

This sector includes individual providers and healthcare institutions. It is hierarchical and includes powerful big business corporations. Providers are the source of most healthcare system bills and payments to the same. We pay more for high-risk, highly complicated healthcare and have miles to go before seriously rewarding preventive, early care, and chronic care management.

In his book *Uncaring*, Robert Pearl (2021, p. 297), former CEO of the Permanente Medical Group, writes, "The first step in solving any problem is admitting one exists. In American medicine, cultural change will only begin when doctors acknowledge and confront their role in making US healthcare the most expensive and least effective system in the developed world."

With its size and legacy, it will take time to change this sector, both within it and with the other four sectors. However, if the five sectors can work together, change is possible and can be sustainable. Every sector will need a voice at the table and will be called upon to bring solutions to the problem.

In this chapter, there are four primary areas to understand:

1. The US has over 7.3 million licensed health care professionals (HCPs) and over six thousand hospitals. Providers are present in every discussion, whether it relates to care delivery, charging for care and getting paid, using the latest drugs, medical tests and treatments, or the passing of laws related to healthcare services.

2. Healthcare delivery models will continue to change to meet the population's need for access and cost-effectiveness. This change includes primary care delivered in various settings and organizational structures with new frameworks:

    ★ Professional training and education changes will begin to satisfy the pent-up demand from consumers and patients.

    ★ Financial incentives also need to accompany these changes.

3. Regarding cost shifting, the billing process is complex, with different rates charged for each payer according to con-tracted agreements:

    ★ The process is controlled by a chargemaster operation run out of the provider's finance department. The bills do not reflect the actual service charges and are often higher than the actual costs of care.

    ★ Billing and payments will continue to be enhanced and changed along with the care delivery models.

4. Provider/payer business models such as Kaiser Permanente and Geisinger that align the incentives of both the provider and payer sectors demonstrate positive outcomes.

5. The Triple Aim may seem designed to address the work of this sector when, in fact, it was created to optimize the healthcare system's performance. Population health is a challenge in a system designed to address individual healthcare needs, but progress is being made in examining and enhancing overall population health services.

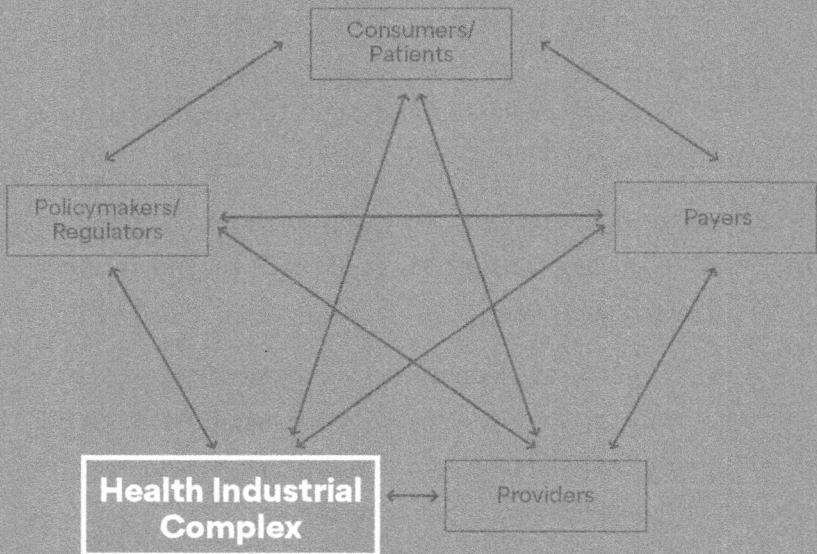

CHAPTER 6

The Health Industrial Complex

The Health Industrial Complex (HIC) is essential, and its history of contributions and its continued role in the growth of the US health system are significant. The HIC is the R&D sector, contributing to many modern healthcare advances. For example, this sector developed antibiotics and vaccines in the first half of the twentieth century. The HIC is the sector that invented the first heart pacemaker in the 1950s. It is the sector that develops and produces varied diagnostic and treatment devices. Robotic surgery has evolved in this sector.

The HIC is the home base sector for the fundamental science of health and medical informatics, electronic records, and similar healthcare efficiencies. It is also where developments around biotechnology and genomics reside. Innovative treatments for cancer, heart disease, and other concerning health conditions spring from here. This sector has contributed to improvements in rural healthcare. Because of this, the HIC is extremely important and influential. Both the Triple Aim and the Hidden Triple Aim are at play.

You have likely read or heard about the HIC's significant money issues and controversies in the media. These include high prices for drugs, overtreatment, waste, and duplicative treatments, many of which are supported by continual innovations in the HIC. Still, you may not have considered how millions of consumers and patients benefit from new and established treatments developed in this sector.

Where would we be without HIC contributions, such as over-the-counter analgesics for minor sore throats or aches from falls or surgical techniques to insert a new orthopedic device? These innovations help people feel better and, in many cases, change lives significantly. Does the press cover this? Not much. However, these advancements are the result of the HIC sector.

In a chapter of the book *Healing Technology* (Kunisch, 1989), I described the HIC as an area of the healthcare system made up of investment-supported research and development (R&D), biotech, medical device production, pharmaceuticals, and informatics. In the thirty years since, there has been tremendous growth and change both within the sector and in its relationships with the other four sectors. I've claimed that the providers sector has seen the most significant change as a result of how healthcare is delivered. But when I consider the HIC, my head spins with the science and developments that are the root of change for the providers in many cases. We are witnessing this sector's ripple effect across all the star sectors.

This sector has three major branches: investment, R&D, and products/services. While it is seemingly different from the other sectors because of its for-profit, taxpaying business models, you should realize by now that the need to make money is universal throughout the star, not just here. Similar to all the sectors, the HIC also shares the focus on health, access, and cost-effectiveness for all: the Triple Aim.

The HIC sector has many start-up companies that have catalyzed innovations across the healthcare system. Think about the daily use of patient care treatments developed in the HIC, including medical devices (e.g., cardiac stents and orthopedic and other implantables), diagnostic and imaging tools, advanced surgical technologies, and pharmaceuticals. HIC-developed informatics and electronic medical record (EMR) platforms and, more recently, AI influence how the sectors provide care and do business. Direct sales to consumers and patients of HIC-developed health and medical management devices, not just pharmaceuticals, have transformed the consumers/patients sector.

The direct relationship between the HIC and the consumers has altered the face of our national health expenditures. Not including pharmaceuticals, we see that 13 percent of health expenditures are now spent on retail outlet sales of medical products, with a projected annual growth rate of more than 5 percent over the next eight years. This growth means that direct-to-consumer and -patient businesses will also continue to grow (Assistant Secretary for Planning and Evaluation—Office of Science & Data Policy, 2002; Keehan et al., 2023; McGough et al., 2023). While some of this growth is attributable to healthcare services for the growing 65+ years segment of the population, other sales growth relates to an increase in the different types of wellness products used by consumers/patients, such as fitness and health status devices. Some of this money comes straight from the consumers' and patients' pockets, so their attention is called to it.

As demonstrated by the amount of time required to develop new products, the HIC is also an area that ensures safety. It is a highly regulated sector to protect consumers and patients. For example, it takes ten years on average for pharmaceuticals to move from the lab to distribution and use by consumers and patients, and this length of time is one of the reasons for the sector's high investment figures. Before sales can begin, money is necessary to sustain these R&D and regulatory processes. While some of the profit money funds future research, other money is available from venture capital investors who continue to invest because, when a drug or treatment becomes a major success, the payback on the investment can be significant. Funding in this sector is essential to ensure that future research and innovations continue to contribute to the advancement of healthcare.

This sector can respond in real time. During the 2020 pandemic, the rush to create a vaccine and deliver it to a global population resulted in a serious examination of the time it takes for the R&D processes and steps to safely bring vaccines to the public. One outcome of this urgency was a shortening of the timeline for product development. It has been suggested that this shortening can be applied across the HIC system. However, this is a regulatory decision, and regulatory bodies are not quick to make this kind of decision.

We agree that developing new medical devices, surgical tools, pharmaceuticals, diagnostic tests, biotechnology, and informatics are vital to healthcare. However, the overall HIC sector can cause frustration for consumers and patients because of the seemingly large profits accumulated by the developers, the direct-to-consumer focus promoting specific medications through advertising and leading consumers and patients to ask for new medicines, and the lengthy R&D timeframes that the public believes are too long, as they do not realize the complexities of the process.

Because of the size and influence of this sector, the media coverage and discussion about it by elected officials often skew what we know. To better understand the sector, let's look at its three components.

Investments

HIC investment is significant, as it supports R&D and new product development. These investments in medical/biotechnology production and distribution comprise an industry that is essential to the

US economy. While we focus here on the US healthcare system, the impact of these investments in this sector is significant worldwide.

There are four categories of HIC investments:

1. *Money coming directly from the HIC sector's profits.* This includes profits from the sale of existing drugs, products, and devices and money from stock sales and value increases of publicly held HIC companies. According to the "Research and Development in the Pharmaceutical Industry" report presented by the Congressional Business Office (2021, April 8), more than 25 percent of new revenues from the sale of existing HIC products were directed to R&D spending in the three years starting from 2019.

2. *Money coming from government investment in R&D.* This includes funds for the National Institutes of Health (NIH), which reached $40 billion in 2020, and the newly launched Advanced Research Projects Agency for Health (ARPA-H), which initially allocated $2.5 billion to set up clinical trials and bring new health products to market (Whyte, 2023).

3. *Money coming from philanthropic funding.* These are often focused on a single disease or population group and direct their investments accordingly.

4. *Money coming from venture capital.* Venture capital is available for new or expanding businesses, many of which are in this sector.

Investment money goes to companies working on basic science or the discovery stage and companies involved in late-stage development, translational development, or clinical trials, which is known as moving from bench science to population benefits. A recent example of late-stage development was developers focusing on the race to find a vaccine during the COVID-19 pandemic, when over a hundred global pharma companies were working on this goal.

This awareness of the importance of HIC investment helps us rethink our biases toward profits and the reinvestment of these monies. Earnings from these developments can be in billions of dollars, with a portion of the earnings returned to the companies' R&D work. Without these investments and a vibrant R&D industry, healthcare innovations would have been delayed.

If we look at the development history of several of the large, well-known, well-established medical device and pharmaceutical companies, we see years of using profits from the companies' sales to design and introduce new patient care products. These products change millions of people's lives worldwide, emphasizing the HIC sector at its best.

However, with these investments come power, control, and money. We read about complex business models with mergers and acquisitions, joint ventures and partnerships, patent disputes, and government oversight. All these issues are reported to the public and, at times, paint a picture we do not like.

At the same time, the HIC is also a home for risk-takers and innovators, and this is unique among the star sectors. It is an environment that encourages creative and entrepreneurial thinking and welcomes newcomers. The biotech area is flush with small companies in genomics, drugs, and medical devices.

These small companies can raise cash, and while larger parent companies acquire some of them, others proceed to initial stock offerings. The source of initial money is venture capital directed to preclinical and clinical researchers. The payoff can be big, whether the company is bought or goes public. Note that most of these companies are located in the US (Thomas & Wessel, 2023). This is one reason why the US health system is so large and powerful.

Research and Development

From bench science to new product launches, the R&D component is the heart of the HIC sector and draws significant investment dollars. Much has been written on this area as science branches into genomics and Artificial Intelligence (AI).

The HIC can collaborate with the providers sector, and providers often come into the industry to develop their ideas for healthcare improvements and frequently make money because of them. The HIC is not a legacy sector that does the same thing year in and year out, so why wouldn't they want to bring their ideas and work with this sector? There is a lot of potential to make big money.

Much of the corporate budget in pharmaceutical or medical device companies goes to R&D, including researching and developing new treatments to improve our health. While the general notion is that they engage in price gouging and pushing their products to consumers, the fact is that new products use the research process guidelines in place to protect the public, and this process is long and expensive. These guidelines and requirements are overseen by the US Food and Drug Administration (FDA), the US Public Health Service, the American Medical Society, institutional research boards (IRBs), and others.

In addition, the legal patenting process is a major step in the R&D process, which requires the publication of the device or pharmaceutical development process. Patent documents are publicly available, and if you choose to read them, you can learn way more than you might anticipate. I was introduced to patent documents while studying the marketing of electronic fetal monitors and the significant increase in cesarean births with the use of the monitors. I learned that the machine's fetal heartbeat measurement was incorrect at times, and the machine was reporting false data at the bedside. It took several years and more patents to correct the problem, and it was a big wake-up call for me.

Because biotech is the focus and locus of so much present-day medical research, it is essential to understand the guidelines and regulations that must be followed for research to be ethically and legally conducted. Much of this regulation development work was done following WWII, resulting in the passage of the National Research Act (NRA) in 1974. Several major transgressions led to the NRA, including the infamous Tuskegee Experiment (CDC, 2021) and, of course, the Nuremberg trials (National WWII Museum, n.d.), which revealed significant abuse of human subjects in medical research experiments.

While these are some of the widely known unethical research instances, there have been others over the years. Also note that at the time of the enactment of the NRA, research monies funded by the federal government had grown significantly, from $117 million in 1950 to $1.86 billion in 1968 (Rice & Cooper, 1970). One of the critical components of the NRA also required voluntary consent for all participants in US medical research funded by federal dollars. In addition, the study design had to be reviewed and approved in advance by an IRB and the newly established National Commission for the Protection of Human Subjects of Biomedical Research (CDC, 2021; HHS, 2022).

Only some believe everything is good in the R&D world. In his book *Code Blue: Inside America's Medical Industrial Complex*, Mike Magee (2019, p. 230) writes a revealing and well-documented chapter on the funding and publication of the results of medical research:

"Bottom line: the American system of research is rife with unethical conduct and financial conflict of interest."

He notes that US companies sponsor drug experiments in other countries with far less strict research guidelines. He further teases out the conflict of interest among physician researchers who do not publish poor results and peer-reviewed articles written by ghostwriters, which are not signed off by a percentage of the study's physician researchers. Controversial? Hidden Triple Aim? You bet. I ask, "Is there something in the HIC's overall structure that allows this to happen?"

HIC Products

The HIC has four major product areas where activity and innovation are ongoing. Within each area, changes take place, resulting in new treatments that can be less expensive, often conducted outside of hospitals, and ultimately more effective. Sitting in the star's center requires us to acknowledge and incorporate these developments into our planning.

BIOTECH

Biotechnology is the future of medicine. It is an applied science integrating natural and engineering sciences. It has grown exponentially along with the growth of informatics technology and biomedical technology. One of the first biotech companies, Genentech, began in 1976 and had a corporate headquarters address of 1 DNA Way and an NYSE symbol of DNA. Talk about being a pioneer.

Biotechnology is an advanced area in medical and health sciences and comes from areas including biology, chemistry, physics, statistics, and genomics, among others. Biotechnology is the area that develops the technologies and products used for preventing and treating diseases. It uses our genetic makeup to diagnose and tailor treatments for individuals to reduce disease rates. It is sophisticated in biological and engineering techniques and methods, making it more precise, measurable, and reproducible.

While Big Pharma, medical device/product companies, and research companies promote biotech products, biotechnology is an industry unto itself. It is an R&D industry specializing in breakthrough therapies. It is the home of gene therapy, immunotherapy, and precision therapy. Biostatistics and bioinformatics are critical components of this industry. While big, established companies have biotechnology work underway, it is an industry populated with start-ups and venture capital. Biotechnology has a significant presence in the US and worldwide.

Biotechnology is an integral part of the health system and the HIC. Medicine biotechnology is a major influence on pharmaceutical and disease treatments in the healthcare system. For example, synthetic insulin has had a significant positive impact on diabetes management since its development in the late 1970s. Genetic testing is another biotechnology specialty area that brings advanced science to diagnoses and treatment processes.

A 2022 report on healthcare biotech R&D companies by the Biotechnology Innovation Organization (BIO) provides several descriptors we can use to understand this industry's size and scope (Thomas & Wessel, 2023). The BIO report looks at the overall medical biotechnology industry worldwide, including investments in preclinical and clinical R&D and major R&D areas. The report shows that the US conducts most biotech work, followed by Asia and Europe. In 2021, venture capital in the US was $25 billion versus $18 billion in Europe, Asia, and the rest of the world combined (Bryan, 2022; Moore, n.d.). Venture capital is big in the R&D space.

Vaccines are on the list of R&D areas, but so are other major biotech areas, including oncology, Parkinson's disease, shingles, neurology, gene editing, and rare diseases. In 2021, small companies were originating and conducting 77 percent, or the majority, of biotech work. Among the companies reviewed in the report were 6,918 clinical pipeline programs under research to eventually reach FDA approval (Thomas & Wessel, 2023). And the number that comes out with approval? Approximately 10 percent (Congressional Budget Office, 2021). That is the size of the biotechnology industry.

BIG PHARMA

Let me repeat: *Big Pharma has benefited humanity on a grand scale and individually.* The pharmaceutical industry has changed lives. It is essential and contributes to world health.

So with 10 percent to 11 percent of annual medical spending (ten to eleven cents of every dollar spent on healthcare) in the category of pharmaceuticals (CMS.gov, 2023d), let's go right up front and address the high costs. There is no doubt this component of the HIC sector is controversial. Yet if there was one thing that opened the eyes of the public to what the pharmaceutical industry does for us, it was the 2020 pandemic, when we had vaccines available within a short period and, later, treatments. It was amazing.

Pharma has always received a lot of attention. Between the news media and elected officials regularly reporting on outrageous drug pricing and advertisements for specific medications, we are exposed to Big Pharma regularly. The reality is that money is required to manufacture, produce, and distribute existing medications and cover the costs of pharmaceutical R&D before we can take advantage of a successful breakthrough drug. As noted, it is expensive to develop new drugs. It takes ten years on average to reach complete approval, starting with development at the bench, followed by five to six years of clinical trials. This results in only one in ten new drugs passing the test. All those years to create new medications add up to millions, if not billions, of dollars spent on the process.

We also know that not all the research money goes into new drugs. Drug companies also invest in finding effective new combinations of existing drugs and new drug-delivery mechanisms, such as insulin pumps. Drug R&D also goes to therapeutic classifications, such as HIV, cancer, and autoimmune diseases, and drugs for relatively large population groups with chronic illnesses requiring continued treatment. It is extensive, complex, and expensive, and as previously noted, most of the research work is done here in the US (Congressional Budget Office, 2021).

The issue of R&D's high cost, a major subject for elected officials and the media, is being addressed by the R&D industry itself. For instance, to continue to innovate yet address high costs, save money, and speed up the testing process, the tissue engineering industry (HIC) is growing replacement organs to provide realistic and more cost-effective R&D testing. Working with regulators to shorten testing periods is another priority, also spurred on by the pandemic vaccine experience.

On the demand side of Big Pharma are the expectations of consumers and patients who believe pharma should be a fix for whatever ails us. There is a widespread dilemma when the wants-versus-needs situation presents itself to HCPs. By this, I mean that when a patient visits with a health problem, they expect providers to prescribe something—or anything. It is complicated to tell a patient, "There is nothing I can do," and writing a prescription eases that dilemma. So demand is a contributing factor to high costs as well.

We also expect new drugs to come out and be an improvement on what we are currently taking. Again, producing new and improved drugs can be costly, and the results are only sometimes what we antici-pate. Side effects, combined with other pharmaceuticals the patient is taking, may contribute to poor outcomes (American Academy of Actuaries, 2018; Donahoe, 2021). It is a highly complex environment, not a cost-saving guarantee.

Other innovations to control costs come from the payers, who work with HCPs to set up drug benefit programs. These formular-ies list safe and efficacious drugs paid for under an insurance plan's prescription drug benefit. The key words here are "safe and efficacious." For a long time, these formularies were solely on the private health insurance side. However, to control expenses, public medical benefit programs, including the passage of Medicare Part D in 2006, were sent to private insurers who set up drug benefit programs. A prescription drug formulary was created for Medicare, Medicaid, or other benefi-ciary programs using the requirements of the private health plan to control costs and provide comprehensive therapeutic treatments.

A further cost in pharmaceuticals is the Pharmacy Benefit Managers (PBM) organization, which secures pharmaceuticals directly from the pharmaceutical producer and acts as an intermediary on behalf of the payers and the pharmacies. PBMs are indeed intermediaries and add a layer of costs. PBMs are part of the distribution process for medica-tions, and while the prices of the drugs available through the PBMs are fixed and procurement is assured, they are blamed for higher costs than direct purchasing. However, with this procurement ability, I am not sure anyone wants to eliminate PBMs in an industry this large.

Unfortunately, the formularies are unique to each payer, and HCPs may prescribe medications without knowing what a formulary looks like, as each one is seemingly different. Sometimes, the direct cost of a medication is more than the patient expected. The result? An unhappy patient.

The resolution of these conflicts, including our unrealistic expectations of what pharma can do for a patient, differing formularies with inconsistent costs for patients, and biased public news or an incomplete picture of how pharma R&D and the pharma approval processes work, will only come from the involvement of all the star sectors. Let's stand at the center of the star. We often observe the conflicts related to power and money across the health system, which always return to the tension between Big Pharma and any negative public relations and the ultimate benefit of R&D's impact on humanity.

MEDICAL DEVICES AND DIRECT-TO-CONSUMER PRODUCTS

Here, we experience real change in the HIC and, ultimately, the health system. In the early years, the HIC sector depended on providers to bring HIC products to consumers and patients when the providers delivered healthcare services. The process of providers ordering and managing the use of medical devices and laboratory tests included testing and treatment at the provider site and some types of testing and monitoring, where the patient took a device home and wore it for a period, and then the data were collected and given to the provider.

Examples include an external monitor for pregnant women, which could monitor any uterine contractions early in pregnancy, or a cardiac monitoring device for patients with hypertension or cardiac arrhythmia. These types of monitoring require a prescription from an HCP and continue today, especially when dealing with highly specialized, complex diagnostic products and devices. However, nowadays, direct-to-consumer, patient wellness, and chronic disease management products, including some pharmaceuticals, specialty medical equipment, and dietary supplements, are delivered straight to consumers/patients through retail outlets. The providers are the third party in the relationship.

An excellent example of this was COVID-19 testing done at home during the pandemic. Several large HIC companies developed self-test kits, which were sold and also distributed free of charge. Providers sometimes complain about direct-to-consumer promotions and sales, but I never heard any complaints about COVID-19 self-testing from the providers.

They were happy to keep the numbers of consumers/patients manageable through self-testing or testing in other sites, such as retail drug stores and pharmacies located in grocery stores. While persons with diabetes test their blood sugar regularly and women purchase over-the-counter pregnancy tests, other types of medical testing were functions "owned" by the providers. Therefore, this change was new, and more of these changes will come about slowly.

Today, not only do we self-*test*, but we also self-*monitor*. The difference? Testing provides data to a healthcare provider, while monitoring provides data for an individual to use to self-manage their health. For example, many people now use their wristbands and watches to track their blood oxygen level, pulse rate, and cardiac output. Wearable devices with optical sensors—so-called smartwatches—are commonly used to measure wearers' pulse rates (Strain et al., 2019).

Algorithms have been developed using pulse wave data to detect atrial fibrillation and atrial flutter (Tison et al., 2018). An Apple Watch application uses intermittent, passively detected pulse rate data in an algorithm to identify episodes suggestive of atrial fibrillation (Apple Inc., 2020). At the time of purchase, the watch wearer is instructed on how to manage themself if there is a change. Moreover, they are instructed on when to call a provider if the self-management steps show no improvement.

These self-monitoring devices are still in development, and patents concerning various tools must be more explicit (Lindwall, 2024). At the time of this writing, there are ongoing disputes about the patents, and specific sensors in the watches have been disabled. This is an example of the late end of a ten-year product development process, when a product's legal ownership is evaluated for compliance.

This is a long way from the past, when physicians and nurses controlled the measurement of such conditions, and consumers and patients were an uninvolved third party. With these successes and the move to population health, self-use technologies focus on managing chronic diseases and maintaining a healthy state. Make no mistake, more of these developments are coming from the HIC, resulting in the need for the other sectors to adjust their communication and treatment practices.

And who is paying for this? Currently, consumers and patients are paying for technological innovations, such as self-monitoring watches. For diagnostic testing, it is the payers. However, in the other sectors, the payers and providers are experimenting with their self-management models, and more change is likely to occur.

Data Collection and Informatics

While health information technology encompasses all the tools, technologies, systems, and processes of collecting, sharing, and storing healthcare data, health informatics focuses on the use and application of these data. As the CDC puts it, health informatics is the source behind the development of health IT.

Health informatics applies concepts, theories, and practices to analyze and present data information for healthcare practitioners to apply to their care of patients and achieve better health outcomes (USF

Health, n.d.). To improve outcomes, we seek to identify at-risk patients and intervene with preventive or early care rather than waiting for high-intensity, high-cost tertiary treatment models. We want to improve access for all, and we need to design, implement, and execute interventions. The data are the source of information that makes this possible.

The most significant change in the past 25+ years is likely the use of electronic medical records (EMRs) and certified electronic health record (EHR) technology. Paper charts are long gone because of the EMR's introduction in the 1970s. EMRs and EHRs became digitized versions of paper charts that contained medical histories, diagnoses, allergies, immunization dates, medications, and physicians' and nurses' notes. It wasn't long before the US health system quickly realized that while EMR and EHR data collection was helpful, a broader version of EMRs and EHRs was necessary.

These health records allowed for incorporating lab results from outside the practice and referrals to other providers, billing payers, communicating among providers, and transferring data according to CMS standards. Also included were decision-making support and greater details on patient demographics. (Some systems now offer a patient portal to enhance communications. It is an extensive record.) Other technologies also entered the health delivery sites, including barcoding medications and patients, which reduced medication errors and improved patient safety.

Just in case you are wondering, in order to protect patient privacy, all these systems, especially when information goes to the payers, need to be approved and be compliant with the Health Insurance Portability and Accountability Act (HIPAA), which was created in 1996 when most health information was on paper.

Several positives come from EMRs and EHRs, including ease of transferring information across various points in the health system, resulting in productivity and efficiency improvements, which are valuable assets. Suppose you have a physical exam and need a follow-up x-ray. In that case, your record is electronically sent to the x-ray office, and the x-ray results are electronically sent back to the prescribing provider.

No paper, no lost information. Furthermore, this adds more data for use in analysis and research. However, these changes to EMRs and EHRs were not easily accepted in a health system this size. Frontline providers had to change their practices, and bringing a computer into the exam room was met with resistance. The amount of data recorded was also frustrating at times, and for many years, EMRs and EHRs were considered a deterrent to patient care, a distraction, and an obligation on a long list of things to do.

While all data collection must be HIPAA compliant, the federal HITECH Act, initially passed in 2009, did not require healthcare providers to convert all medical charts to a digital format until 2014 (CMS.gov, 2023a). In addition, as part of HITECH, CMS provided incentives to meet requirements for meaningful use (data collection designed to be meaningful and useful). Providers received financial penalties on their reimbursements for failing to meet the EMR and EHR adoption criteria.

Hardship exemptions were allowed. However, the goals of quality of care, enhanced care coordination, and support for decision-making were a priority. Over a period of years, the transition to EMRs and EHRs was accomplished, and with the demonstrated greater efficiency and meaningful use of data, electronic records became accepted. Do you see the time this took?

Additionally, the federal government established the Office of the National Coordinator for Health Information Technology to oversee the implementation and use of health IT and electronic health information exchange. Know that HIPAA and HITECH work together, with HIPAA covering all health information and HITECH focusing on the electronic components of health information.

With the transition to electronic medical and health records, the race was on to create and sell a comprehensive product. Today, the largest EMR and EHR companies are CureMD, Athenahealth, Epic, AdvancedMD, and Cerner (Jamble, 2024). These companies employ technical staff backup systems and continually work with healthcare providers, national payers, and regulatory agencies to ensure compliance and cybersecurity. As of this writing, Cerner and Epic are the largest, with revenue streams of billions of dollars. It is a big business and a competitive marketplace.

Yet we must be cautious when using data. Although we can capture and better analyze data from many different sources, including EMRs and EHRs, we must be careful with our goals and boundaries. Data protection and use are the next bastions of innovation, and they are critical.

Personally Collected Health Data

Consider the identification and use of personally collected health data. The Fitbit wristband, for example, collects data on heart rate, activity, calories taken in, hydration and tracks sleep. It is a company owned by Google, which also owns the Pixel Watch, which collects health data.

In terms of privacy, because the device is owned and used by an individual and collects data on an individual basis, if the data on one's watch is accessed, this can potentially be a serious problem. The Fitbit privacy policy is clear on what is collected by Fitbit and the use of the data (Google Fitbit, n.d.), and it is a strong case for "buyer beware."

Fitbit owners must read and understand the policies. They are about their health information.

Collecting and managing one's health data is interesting. However, the HIPAA privacy and health information protection laws were written and put into practice over twenty-five years ago, and HITECH was put into law over fifteen years ago. Data mining is provocative and extremely informative, and the geniuses at work are making important discoveries.

What uses this information will have is the question. This data collection is happening now, and personal health information protection laws have yet to keep up with the technology. There is a lot of good to come out of this data collection, both at the bench in the early development of new treatments and population health work. However, a literal danger to one's personal property exists.

Currently, neither the healthcare providers nor the payers have anything to do with the data collected on these personal devices. The key phrase in that last sentence is "right now" because, with the collection of this personalized health information, the opportunities to use the data to manage one's health are coming, and the HIC is becoming directly involved with health services.

Artificial Intelligence

At the time of this writing, AI remains a potential healthcare delivery tool giving access to vast amounts of readily available information. Experts say that until there are knowledge-based AI systems that can reason, decide, and explain decisions, AI will be an information tool, not a professional decision-maker. Indeed, AI brings together many facts and offers new perspectives on illnesses and treatments. Yet many experts exploring how

AI will work on the front lines agree that there is work to be done to make it usable in diagnosis and treatment (Hood & Price, 2023).

Robert Pearl (2024, March 25) offers three ways "generative AI's improved memory will transform patient care": more accurate diagnoses, fewer complications from chronic diseases, and safer hospitals. While Pearl agrees there is still work to do before these become a reality, he is optimistic concerning the opportunities and the benefits to patients and providers alike. He projects significant savings in lives and dollars related to improved care management, keeping patients at less acute stages that are, therefore, less costly. However, with the noted emphasis on specialization in medicine, how well will this happen, or how quickly will it happen? And what is the role of AI relative to each patient?

Another example of work using AI is suicide prevention. Mental health experts and researchers are studying AI as a tool for assessing suicide risk. A review of the literature in 2022 concluded that AI has a high potential for identifying patients at risk of suicide. At the time, algorithms in clinical situations required further development and clarification.

Ethics, too, have played a major role in the development process, including issues around informed consent and privacy. It is a challenging undertaking and highly complex, and AI is only a part of the process (Lejeune et al., 2022). AI is a paramount issue and is both a major opportunity and a major threat. Frontline providers—the people making the decisions concerning patient care—are rightly cautious.

So if you want to create effective change, be patient and keep learning.

Summary

The HIC is the sector that is the source of much of the product development in healthcare delivery, including treatments and pharmaceuticals. It is a dynamic sector that is responsive in real time and is the source of new cutting-edge treatments. It is also the center for data collection and informatics related to the healthcare system and specific products.

The HIC works closely with healthcare providers and is developing direct-to-consumer products. It is a sector with many start-up companies and long-established major research and product development entities. While we want to think this is all in the future, when we examine this sector, in many cases, the future is now.

There are three major branches in this sector, each with various parts:

1. Investments essentially provide the necessary capital to conduct research and develop products. These funds come from various sources, including profits from the sale of existing products, research dollars, government investments, philanthropic funding, and venture capital.

2. R&D is the heart of the HIC sector, with new product developments and current product improvements operating within ethical and regulatory guidelines and regulations. The timeline to take a new product from the science bench to full approval and practice is generally ten years. And the rate of success in the number of new products

reaching this final place is frequently only 10 percent. Additional product developments modify existing devices or medications. These initiatives can add enhancements and expand the therapeutic benefits of already completed work. The process is regulated and shortens the period to deliver an enhanced product into practice.

3. There are four main areas of product development impacting the delivery of healthcare services in the US: bio-technology, pharmaceuticals, medical devices and direct-to-consumer products, and health data collection and informatics. As a result of these developments, the overall healthcare system has grown, showing that the HIC plays a significant role in ensuring that healthcare is ever-changing for the benefit of the population.

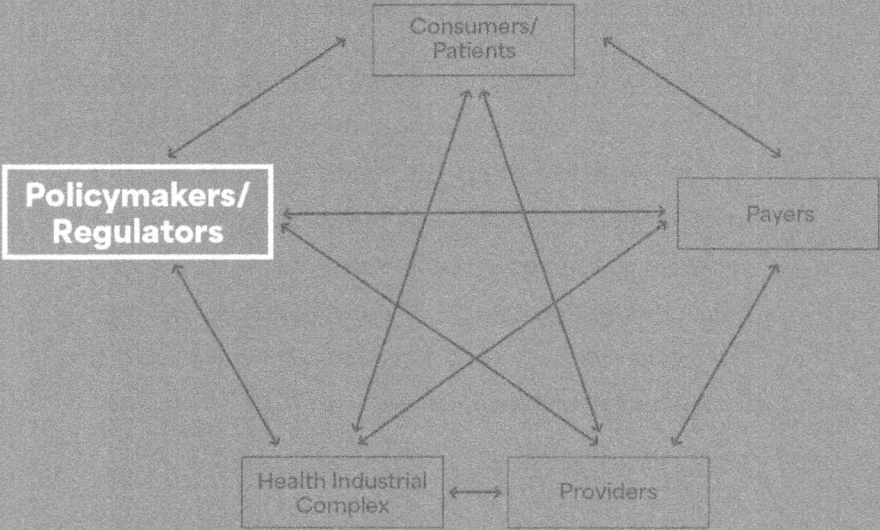

CHAPTER 7

Policymakers

Policymaking. The public sector. Bureaucracy. Power, control, and money. When you think of the policy sector, you may envision elected officials, government agencies and regulations, bills such as the Patient Protection and Affordable Care Act (ACA), lobbyists working on an agenda, and major government-payer programs, such as Medicare and Medicaid.

You should also include think tanks and commissions advising on solutions to health issues that affect the American people, as well as taxpayers and voters, because both influence what happens in the policy sector. It is a large and complex sector—a place of power, control, and money, not to mention the ensuing conflicts. The media regularly reports on issues in this sector, so we often know more about this sector than the private businesses in the payers, providers, and health industrial complex (HIC) sectors.

All this government work takes money, the source of which are taxes and taxpayers, and tax money is not a never-ending source of money. The Triple Aim goals of cost-effective health services and demonstrated quality of care are critically important when spending tax dollars. Here are a few highlights on the taxpayer-funded federal budget. In 2023, the federal budget was $6.1 trillion.

In 2023, the federal government mandated the health spending budget to be $1.45 trillion, with an additional $231 billion for a discretionary health budget, bringing the total to $1.68 trillion, or 27.5 percent of the federal budget (Cubanski et al., 2023). Much of this money went to Medicare, Medicaid, CHIP, and the ACA subsidies. These numbers represent the largest category of budgeted federal spending. Interestingly, in 2019, healthcare spending was 30 percent of a $4.45 trillion federal budget. So while the federal budget grew by 37 percent, healthcare spending grew by 20 percent during COVID-19, when the system focused on high-risk and sick patients. This shows the impact of COVID-19 pandemic spending programs on overall federal spending (Ready et al., 2023).

The policy sector plays a vital role in the US healthcare system. Its function is to promote and provide for the general welfare of the population, as written in the Constitution's preamble and article I. While the Constitution was written in simpler times and certainly before our current US healthcare system was ever imagined, today, the government has several roles that address the general welfare of the population.

These include regulating a $4.9 trillion healthcare delivery system, ensuring access and safety, paying for the care of some people, and, at times, directly providing care through government-sponsored health-care delivery institutions. Today, the healthcare system's policy sector includes federal and state governments and sometimes local governments because, like everything else in the US in the last 200+ years, the government has grown and expanded too.

In most cases, the government protects the general welfare of consumers and patients not by providing direct care but by controlling aspects of the direct care system. They do this through policymaking and passing healthcare-related laws in the legislative branches at both the federal and state government levels. These laws are executed and regulated through the government bureaucracy.

Once legislators at both the federal and state levels have passed laws, the policy sector creates bureaucracies that serve as administrators of the legislation. The role of these bureaucracies is to assess the need for services related to the laws, provide funding to establish and sometimes provide the needed services, and conduct regulatory oversight. Federal and state healthcare system policies, laws, and bureaucracies are part of our everyday reality. The laws passed at these levels address many topics, including safety, access, and cost-effectiveness. It is the Triple Aim at work.

When we want to see change in the healthcare system, we can be sure policy and the government will be involved in the change efforts. Healthcare system spending is the largest category in the federal budget. After passing laws and establishing service delivery, bureaucratic government regulation focuses on public safety, including bureaucratic oversight related to providers, by governing healthcare service delivery and professional licensing. It also focuses on the HIC's oversight of R&D in medical technologies and devices, pharmaceuticals, health informatics, and bureaucracies related to the payers, including oversight of private health insurance plans to ensure that the insurance companies will not run out of money to meet their financial obligations when there is a need to pay for the care of insured people.

A recent example of this is the Inflation Reduction Act of 2022 (Cubanski et al., 2024). This extensive federal act covers healthcare costs and ensures savings on pharmaceuticals for seniors on Medicare and an extension for three more years of health insurance premium savings originally in the Affordable Care Act (ACA).

These savings include reductions in private insurance premiums based on gross income and allow more people to purchase health insurance. It is part of the successful effort to reduce the number of uninsured Americans.

A Closer Look at the Bureaucracies

There is one federal Congress and fifty state legislatures creating policies and laws. Bureaucracies, including federal agencies and commissions, state agencies and commissions, and even local governments, comprise a significant part of this policy sector. An example of a sizable federal health bureaucracy is the US Department of Health and Human Services (HHS), which has eighty thousand employees within eleven operating divisions.

There are other bureaucratic departments at the federal level that involve health system oversight, including the Drug Enforcement Administration (DEA) and the Federal Trade Commission, which attempts to protect competition. Within every state government, there is also a state bureaucracy dedicated to promoting and providing for the general welfare of the population through their state departments of public health, insurance commissions, health professionals, and institutional licensing, among others. The legislative and government administrative functions reach the other four sectors of the star through these bureaucracies.

Bureaucracy provides for public safety through regulations. Regulatory responsibilities include both oversight as well as mandatory reviews. An example is licensing health professionals and health delivery institutions and services. Federal and state departments issue the licenses.

To provide direct healthcare services, one must have a license and be in good standing. To obtain a license, one must have graduated from an accredited institution and have taken and passed an examination sponsored by the licensing bureau. A license certifies the appropriate level of one's professional education and training and specialty area, such as nursing, medical, dental, pharmacy, physical or occupational, respiratory therapy, or psychological therapies.

Institutions, too, must be licensed, including hospitals, nursing homes, assisted living, hospices, surgery centers, diagnostic and laboratory centers, and professional home care. Depending on the type, licensing is done by both the state and federal governments. State and federal health departments have licensing bureaus that administer licensing exams, issue licenses, renew licenses, and receive and address formal complaints. They can also revoke a license regarding care provided by an individual practitioner who cannot practice their profession with reasonable skill or safety. These government departments have similar oversight of healthcare institutions.

While this all sounds simple, the addition of state oversight adds complexities. A national practice level would reduce such complexities. Physicians and dentists have this, but for other professional groups, the states get very involved in legislating the scope of practice or perhaps merely managing the practice requirements.

To understand some of the complexities, one might ask these licensing questions. Do I need a license to be a dentist and care for oral health? Yes. Do I need a license to sell a fitness and exercise calculator wristband? No. However, if the wristband monitors medical conditions and reports them to a healthcare provider, it must be approved by the Food and Drug Administration (FDA) as a form of licensure.

Do I need a license to make a cardiac stent for a clinician to insert into a patient? Yes and yes. The FDA must approve the stent and stipulate that an appropriately licensed HCP can insert the stent. A similar process occurs with prescription drugs. The FDA must approve the drug, and only licensed HCPs with state-approved prescriptive authority can prescribe the drug. For controlled substances, the federal government—the DEA—approves who can prescribe these substances. Then, for all prescriptions, the pharmacist who fills the prescription must also be licensed.

Here is an inconsistency in the process, which circumvents the federal Supremacy Clause in which federal laws passed for national implementation can override state laws. Go back to the Constitution, this time article VI, paragraph 2, which states that federal law generally takes precedence over state laws and even a state constitution.

So the federal government lists the scope of practice requirements for professional licenses, and then the states add regulatory stipulations related to the execution of practice. An example is advanced nurse practitioners and midwives who are licensed according to national criteria. While accepting the federal scope of practice for the profession, the execution of caring for consumers and patients is regulated by the states.

In one state, nurse practitioners and midwives can practice independently, and if they stay within the guidelines written in the practitioner license, this is legal. However, in the state next door, the state legislature has passed a law that nurse practitioners and midwives can only practice under the guidance of a physician. They still follow the federal licensing guidelines, but the state-legislated practice rules are set up to control the practice. This makes no sense and is an example of state versus federal rulemaking.

In the prescriptions for controlled substances example above, the FDA is part of the federal HHS, and the DEA is under the US Department of Justice and is not part of HHS. So while government bureaucracies have a great deal of responsibility and there are a lot of initials and departments, there also needs to be more clarity about who is in charge or where the buck stops.

Another form of consumer/patient protection is the oversight of private insurance companies. To get this job done, state-specific insurance commissions establish and oversee essential requirements, such as the size of insurance risk pools, monetary reserve requirements, and private insurance premium increases. The state insurance commission must approve private insurance premiums, which the payers cannot arbitrarily raise.

With the states responsible for a portion of the Medicaid funding for their state, with the cost shift to private payers and Medicaid being the lowest payer, and with increasing private insurance premiums to cover these extra costs and keep the risk pools liquid, insurance commissions ultimately have a limited course of action except to "approve within reason" these premium increases.

At the federal level, there are initiatives through CMS that cover such items as the No Surprises Act and the federal Inflation Reduction Act, both of which address pharmaceuticals for seniors. This is yet another example of federal legislation directly impacting the payers, no matter the state or the type of payer.

In a health system this large, with fifty state governments and the federal government, there will be duplication on the one hand and a lack of oversight on the other. For the other sectors, keeping track can be confusing and costly.

Government Entitlement Programs

Next, we arrive at purchasing care—the government commitment to pay for healthcare purchases on behalf of specific populations. These payment programs are known as entitlement programs, and the consumers and patients covered are the beneficiaries. Currently, in Medicare (covering senior citizens and people with disabilities),

Medicaid (covering the medically indigent), the Child Health Insurance Program (CHIP), and other government-funded programs, including the Veterans Administration, the Indian Health Service, and Military Health System, the consumers and patients may pay a portion for their care. It is not a free lunch for all.

Many think Medicare is a free ride for its beneficiaries. However, in case you are not aware, unless someone is medically indigent and covered by both Medicare and Medicaid, most Medicare beneficiaries pay co-pays and coinsurance, just like in private health insurance plans. Like everyone else, Medicare beneficiaries pay a monthly premium to Medicare for their coverage.

This premium deduction is taken from an individual's Social Security earnings and adjusted according to their adjusted gross income reported on federal tax forms. Medicare beneficiaries filing with a higher income pay a higher monthly Medicare premium. People who receive a public employee pension payment and not a Social Security check pay a monthly fee directly to Medicare for their coverage. And yes, this is adjusted for gross income, with higher gross income earners paying more.

Additionally, for certain Medicare benefits, beneficiaries must pay a co-pay and possibly coinsurance. So what do many Medicare beneficiaries do because of the Medicare deductions, co-pays, and coinsurance? They purchase coverage out of their pockets: Medigap insurance coverage, Medicare Part D pharmacy, and additional coverage from a private insurer to cover the costs Medicare will not pay. This is not cheap, and it is not a free ride.

There is no risk pool per se for these government entitlement programs. It is just an annual budgeted amount. Medicare, Medicaid, and CHIP are part of the mandatory federal budget, while the other health programs are in the federal discretionary budget (Congressional Budget Office, 2024). So the taxpayers hold the risk, and taxes will increase if healthcare costs increase. If things get exceptionally expensive, the government can add the costs to the national debt, which we are warned about occasionally.

Finally, public hospitals and community-based federally qualified outpatient health centers are healthcare provider institutions that have government money supplementing their budgets and costs. Public hospitals operate some of the most well-known and well-respected institutions in the US today, yet their direct reach through care has lessened over the decades. In 2019, 22 percent of US hospitals were public facilities operated by a hospital district, a city, a county, or a city–county partnership. This list includes the hospitals of the VA, the Department of Defense Military Health System, and the Indian Health Service, which provide direct care to their beneficiaries. All these public hospitals and other services are considered safety nets and essential providers that deliver high-quality care, especially to the vulnerable, and the government financially subsidizes them all.

These hospitals are often located in large cities and administered through the local, state, or federal government. Examples include Jackson Memorial Hospital in Miami, Memorial Hermann Southwest Hospital in Houston, University of Alabama at Birmingham Hospital, and the Ohio State University Wexner Medical Center.

Federally qualified health centers (FQHC) are outpatient services in underserved areas. These community-based providers have a relationship with the Health Resources and Services Administration (HRSA), an agency of HHS. Their purpose is to provide primary care and improve access, regardless of source of or ability to pay. A qualified FQHC receives, in addition to oversight guidance from HRSA, enhanced reimbursements from Medicare and Medicaid to cover operating costs, and it offers patients healthcare fees on a sliding scale (FQHC Associates, n.d.).

Funding Research to Improve Care

A significant role of the government is to directly fund healthcare research and ensure improvements to protect the public's general welfare while caring for its population. As seen in the HIC chapter, government-funded research is essential. Entities such as the NIH and the CDC conduct research and fund R&D in the HIC sector, the providers sector, and even the consumers/patients sector.

These government dollars are significant and support rigorous research. A report by *Research! America* (2022) notes that the US federal government accounts for 25 percent of all US medical and health R&D, spending $61.5 billion. In 2020, the NIH alone accounted for 20 percent ($48.9 billion) of spending in academia through private institutions, businesses, and not-for-profit special interest groups, among others. And now, with the newly launched federal Advanced Research Projects Agency for Health (ARPA-H), there is another $2.5 billion to support government research spending (Whyte, 2023).

Think Tanks and Commissions

There is more to the policymakers sector than government bureaucracy and funding. Some influencers are critical parts of creating change because of their credibility. A few think tanks located in Washington, DC, are the Brookings Institution, the Heritage Foundation, the Cato Institute, and the Urban Institute.

These think tanks greatly influence policymakers and are a potential resource for creating change. Their staff includes scholars who conduct research on specific subjects and publish their research, which is then distributed to policymakers and lobbying entities. Most think tanks are not for profit and are funded by private donations and grants, except in cases where they conduct research on behalf of a government entity and are financed by government funds.

Another influencer in the policy sector is congressional commissions. Congress establishes these formal groups to provide independent advice, make recommendations for changes in public policy, study or investigate a particular problem or event, or perform a specific duty. Commissions are either nonpartisan or bipartisan, with the intent that the findings and recommendations will be more politically acceptable in Congress and to the public.

Commissions are temporary, and while no legal definition exists for what constitutes a congressional commission, there are several conditions under which they exist. A congressional commission is a multimember independent entity that Congress establishes and that exists temporarily, serves in an advisory capacity, is appointed in part or whole by members of Congress, and sends its reports to Congress (Congressional Research Service, 2017).

Information from both think tanks and commissions is released to the public and is useful in policymaking, as well as in creating the rules and regulations that go along with policy.

Lobbyists

Lobbying efforts attempt to influence government actions through communication with legislators and members of regulatory agencies. Lobbyists belong to different categories. Some lobbyists are paid directly by the industry they represent for their lobbying expertise and services. Others, as part of their job descriptions, perform lobbying on behalf of their organizations and often have offices near the government. One example is the senior officers of the American Association of Retired Persons (AARP), which has its executive offices less than a ten-minute walk from the US Capitol building in Washington. Other lobbyists are volunteers and are generally quite specific to a cause connected to a particular legislative action.

A few thoughts on lobbyists. They are powerful and often represent large sums of money that can be brought in for campaign contributions. They can deliver votes to candidates for election or reelection, as well as support for seated elected officials in exchange for favoritism from the elected officials for the lobbyists' agenda. Lobbyists are influential in getting their messages across. They operate at both the federal and state levels and work to influence elected officials and chief bureaucratic appointees. This is the reality, and at times, it is hard to fathom how this meets the original mission of the US Constitution—promoting and providing for general welfare.

Recall the three major congressional health acts that came into being over a sixty-year period, discussed in chapter 2. Why did it take so long to pass these major legislative actions? The answer is that it was due to the tension within our great big system, the dynamics of the elected officials, and the power and money as seen through the screen of the lobbyists. Lobbyists were involved in all three health acts.

According to OpenSecrets.org (2024) and the Center for Responsive Politics, the pharmaceutical, health products, and hospital industries spent over $620 million in 2022, lobbying to influence policymakers' thinking, and that was not a major election year. These industries also spend money on such activities as advertising and campaign contributions (within governmental limits).

Among the largest spenders on lobbying activities are health-care organizations, such as the American Hospital Association, the Pharmaceutical Research and Manufacturers of America, American Health Insurance Plans, the Biotechnology Innovation Organization, and AARP. These organizations represent all of the star sectors, and everyone is involved.

The Biotechnology Innovation Organization (2024), an example of a lobbying organization, claims its purpose is to design and advocate for public policies that represent the best interests of its members. Their efforts break down barriers and reduce bureaucratic hurdles in the healthcare regulatory and reimbursement sectors.

Lobbying is a lawful action with a code of ethics that includes conflict of interest guidelines. Because lobbying is a registered act, you can quickly learn how much money an organization spends each year for lobbying by searching the internet. If you are a member of an organization, you can look at its financials. If you are not a member, websites such as OpenSecrets.org, a nonpartisan, independent, nonprofit research group that tracks money in US politics, can provide you with that information.

If you are visiting Washington, DC, and are interested in these influencers, take a stroll down K Street and Massachusetts Avenue Northwest. Many of the major think tanks and lobbying organizations have their headquarters in these neighborhoods. You will see their buildings and their proximity to legislators and one another.

Summary

The policy sector is multifaceted, and the size and complexity of the roles of elected officials, bureaucrats, taxpayers, consumers, and patients add to the complexity. Unlike three of the other four sectors, the policy sector is not run like a business. There is a flow of money into a budget; however, the money is not earned in the traditional definition of the word. Since the US Constitution was written, and throughout its interpretation over the decades, the policy sector has maintained and grown its presence.

If we move our perspective to the star's center, we see policy as a part of the system but not the whole system. Like some providers, some policy affiliates believe they should control the health system. However, similar to the other sectors that think the same thing, that would not work. The star has five equal sectors. It is not a ladder with one sector outranking another.

Another point about this sector is the attention from the media. We are regularly informed about the work happening in the policy sector. Because of the size of the healthcare system and its relevance to the population, there is much media coverage of policy and the healthcare system. One can find the Triple Aim and Hidden Triple Aim everywhere:

1. Federal and state government legislation drives this sector. Federal and state tax dollars finance it.

2. Bureaucracies are designed to administer laws, ensure patient safety, and allocate and spend tax dollars.

3. Additional public spending is incurred through government payers and included in the federal mandatory and discretionary annual budgets and state budget allocations.

4. Research dollars are critical for the healthcare industry, and much research work is supported by tax dollars.

5. Think tanks and congressional commissions are in place to study and advise legislators on specific health-related topics.

6. Lobbyists are specific in their missions to influence the legislative process. Lobbying is a lawful action with a code of ethics and conflict of interest guidelines.

We can and should work with this sector because it listens and can be the most responsive—we hope.

Consumers/
Patients

Legislatures

Policymakers/
Regulators

Bureaucracies

Think Tanks
& Lobbyists

Gov't

Private
Insurance/
Employers/
Unions

Payers

Self-Pay

Investment
$$$$

Biotech
Pharma
Medical Devices
Informatics

Health Industrial
Complex

Providers

Research &
Development

Facilities/
Agencies

Healthcare
Professionals

PART 3
Star Interplay

In this section, we revisit the star and look at the relationships between the five sectors. Part 2 discussed each sector individually, and this is where we realize that the sectors all have relationships with one another. Here the system diagram includes the various parts of each of the sectors, as described in part 2. Many people want to suggest changes to fix the health system by focusing on only one or two sectors.

However, as noted throughout this book, a change in one or two sectors impacts all five sectors eventually. Without planning for how a change may affect the other sectors, when a change does occur, there can be a disruption.

It is possible to see the relationships between the sectors while viewing the overall system from the star's center and using a systems thinking approach. When we think of change, systems thinking enables us to consider the relationships with the other sectors in the healthcare system, as shown in the arrows, and the possible effects of the change. Change can be good, or it might cause conflict.

With various stakeholders who seemingly have different priorities and complex organizational structures within the sectors, Gerzon (2006) notes that by employing systems thinking, we can understand the relationships between the sectors and identify the significant elements that may be related to potential conflicts. We can also track the conflicts already in play and work more positively when we think across all the sectors that make up the star.

The US healthcare system, with a projected $4.9 trillion spent in 2024 (CMS.gov, 2023e), is an industry with five working sectors delivering healthcare services to a population of 339+ million people. Yet despite its enormity, the healthcare system touches our lives on a very personal level. Currently, there are four major issues. These are the struggles with the overall health of our population, the costs of care, the introduction of a consumer healthcare focus, and the influence of AI. These issues are described as paramount and deserve significant attention, as they strike a chord for many people and receive focused coverage from the media and elected officials.

Additionally, the complexity of some of the issues in a healthcare system this size can often be described as wicked problems. These types of problems crop up when organizations have to face constant change or unprecedented challenges occurring in a social context and when there is disagreement among the stakeholders. It is the social complexity of wicked problems, as well as their technical difficulties, that make them tough to manage (Camillus, 2008).

Major issues, whether wicked or not, consume a lot of attention in a sector's work—work that may not be visible to the public at large. But behind closed doors, there are conversations, problem-solving, and sometimes changes. And know that the more perplexing the issue, the longer it can take for change to be seen and experienced. The slow speed of change reflects the size of the industry.

Most work in the US healthcare system is successful, so when things seemingly do not work well and fail to meet expectations, they get attention—sometimes a *lot* of attention. Remember this when you read about the interrelationships and paramount issues in this section of the book. And remember, while each sector plays a unique role, they all work to support the Triple Aim, and yet all the sectors have issues related to the Hidden Triple Aim. That is the reality.

CHAPTER 8

Healthcare Systems Thinking

Sustainable change is as much about the interplay between the sectors as about the sectors themselves: the relationships and dynamics. Here, dynamics describe the inherent structures and influences of power existing between individuals and groups within a given context. They represent the process of activity, growth, and change. Dynamics can include influences, dominance, privileges, and communication styles (Cambridge Dictionary, 2024). They are present everywhere. Yet when we look at the healthcare system, we may or may not consider the dynamics.

If you are not employed by one of the sectors in the healthcare system, do you think everyone works together, or do you assume they always disagree? Or maybe it is somewhere in between—appreciation followed by frustration, followed by gratitude, and on and on. A good model of how the sectors work together is seen here in my comments on Big Pharma.

Consider that, in addition to most patients, many people working in the system greatly value what the pharmaceutical industry has done and continues to do for patient care and outcomes. Pharmaceuticals are often a major part of the treatment plan and a significant part of helping patients get well. Unfortunately we rarely see this in the media. Yet a major reason for the success of Big Pharma is all five sectors working together. The HIC develops the drugs, the FDA approves the drugs, the providers use the drugs as part of the treatment plans, the payers pay for the treatments, and the consumers/patients take their medications. They come together to provide healthcare. It is the healthcare system working together.

If you are employed in one of the sectors, have you ever worked with teams in another sector? Where do you get your information about the other sectors? Some people are too busy to even think outside their own sector.

Many people do not understand the connections and realities of the healthcare system as an industry or their sector as a business. Without a systems thinking perspective, executing great ideas in only one sector can lead to wondering why the change does not last. Arrow interplay dynamics—connecting, conversing, and forming relationships—are where we can find stories related to change.

These stories show what works and what does not work. There are stories about thinking from the center of the star and otherwise. There are successes and nonsuccesses because, in reality, there are very few total failures—just incomplete changes without long-lasting success. And that is unfortunate.

When the Sectors Don't Work Together

If you are wondering how the five sectors and the arrows work in our healthcare system, picture this: a small examining room in an outpatient setting, about a hundred square feet, with a patient, maybe an accompanying family member or patient advocate, a health care professional (HCP), and perhaps a second HCP. Four people are crowded into a cramped space.

There's a good chance you may have played one of these roles. Yet, while only four people are in that examining room, many more bodies than meets the eye are in there. They, too, influence what is happening right there, and if they are not working from the star's center, the results can be problematic for the four people in the room.

Who are they? The US Congress, the US Supreme Court, state legislators and justices, the administrators and employers of a $4.9 trillion service industry, a payer spending government or private dollars, and pharmaceutical manufacturers. They all hover over the four people in the exam room, influencing the encounter between the patient and the provider and its outcome through the dynamics of policymaking, paying for care, and developing new treatments, pharmaceuticals, and technologies.

It is the five-sector star framework in action. Throughout my career, I have seen the interplay, or lack thereof, between the sectors in all its chaotic glory. Let me illustrate how things can go wrong with three examples.

This first example illustrates how the absence of systems thinking left a successful, well-intentioned program in the lurch when funding ran out. The program had multiyear grants from major funders to support a preterm birth prevention program targeting a group of low-income, at-risk pregnant moms in a city with the fourth-highest infant mortality rate in the US.

In six sites across the city, the program started a preventive care model with a pregnant mother before early labor could begin. The program demonstrated significant and measurable success in patient outcomes. But one day, we realized that when the grants ran out, there was insufficient money in the budgets of the six clinical sites to cover the additional staff we had hired to provide this care.

Unfortunately, we had no idea or plan to convert the grant funding to hard dollars to continue this essential care for these women. Without systems thinking, the interconnectedness between the providers, the payers, and, ultimately, the patients was in danger of losing a successful treatment model. We were working so hard to implement the program that we had not considered a plan for the future. We were working within our sector alone without thinking about the payers and the policy sector bureaucrats.

A second example involves legislators prematurely removing state funding before new funding sources were available. A state-funded program was supporting low-income women (uninsured and under-insured) through a breast and cervical cancer early detection program. Bureaucrats downsized the program's financing in anticipation of increased insurance coverage from the Affordable Care Act (ACA).

What happened? There was a reduction in state money that supported the cancer early detection program, and the new ACA insurance programs for low-income people were enacted and executed slowly. State legislators prematurely interpreted the federal legislation without understanding what this meant in delivering care to patients and having it paid for. Providers were forced to shut down one service while waiting for financing to pay for it from another source. As a result, there was a 65 percent decrease in women served by this pre-vention program within five years (Becker & Mustafa, 2022). Who did that help? The shortsighted failure to understand the intercon-nectedness between policy, providers, and payers caused a lack of screening for two significant diseases with possible downstream health effects in a vulnerable population.

The third example shows the introduction of new technology developed by the health industrial complex (HIC) without a coordinated view across the sectors to plan for using the device in the sectors for which it was intended. During the planning process, any manufacturer of a healthcare device, such as one intended for chronic condition disease management and self-care, needs to consider how readily consumers and patients can adapt to the technology and how easily providers can use the information to manage patient care.

Without executing a coordinated plan for use across the sectors, these devices often remain on the shelf, as it is unclear how to integrate them into the consumers' and patients' daily lives and the providers' healthcare services. Introducing essential healthcare technology is more complex than launching a product, even in the direct sales-to-consumers and -patients market. We have seen products get pulled off the market because the technology was too sophisticated for everyday use, and there was no coordination.

The interconnection of the HIC, the consumers, the patients, and the providers ensures the technology's successful deployment. The providers need to be at the planning table, and once they are there, the payers will come on board, as will the policymakers for product clearance. What are the dynamics when no one is talking to anyone else? Potentially valuable products sit on the shelf.

When systems thinking is not employed, these types of missteps happen frequently in an industry as large as healthcare. If you work in the healthcare system, you may have been part of creating change and then watched in frustration as it did not continue, perhaps because no one knew how to pay for it or there was no money or plan to execute it. These are structural problems created by the convoluted dynamics of the health system.

What does this mean? As shown in the examples above, plans for continued financing are essential, and leaders should work with frontline operations to understand the priorities for care and the impact on healthcare service delivery in line with government payer policy changes. Technology industries should also work with healthcare providers and consumer and patient representatives to plan and execute new technological devices or treatment models.

Examining the arrows representing the interplay, interconnectedness, and involvement of teams from the sectors across the star, we also see that discord is possible between sectors and within sectors. Discord can be significant and represent issues related to power and status, legacy controls, and the money flow—the Hidden Triple Aim.

An example of how power and control in the policymakers/regulators sector influence the providers sector centers around clinical practice authority and differing state policy rules concerning the scopes of practice of physicians, advanced practice nurse practitioners, and midwives. All physicians, dentists, nurse practitioners, and midwives have a single national standard of care. However, there are differences between each specialty's standards of care and standards for scope of practice.

Physicians and dentists have a national scope of practice standard, while nurse practitioners and midwives do not. Instead of a national standard, each state has a unique scope of practice standards for nurse practitioners and midwives, resulting in inconsistent workforce practices and quality of care nationwide and the creation of unnecessary red tape.

In January 2013, the renowned health economist Uwe Reinhardt testified at a subcommittee hearing of the US Senate Committee on Health, Education, Labor, and Pensions that because physicians and dentists have a single national scope of practice standard, there should similarly be a single national scope of practice for nurse practitioners and midwives who are advanced clinicians. In his testimony, Reinhardt noted that these individual state controversies take valuable time and energy away from everyone's work, including state legislators, HCPs, consumers, and patient advocates.

Despite the increasing need for patient care services and the negative impact of providing care with these restrictions, the scope of practice for nurse practitioners and midwives has remained under each state's control. This is a perfect example of how the Hidden Triple Aim—control and power—influences the dynamics between the healthcare sectors.

A second example of the Hidden Triple Aim illustrates the dynamics of power and control in the pharmaceutical pricing system. Here, the HIC stands outside of the health system. The brand name prescription drug reimbursement model is different from the reimbursement models for healthcare services.

Drug pricing models are strictly part of the business model and are covered separately in private health insurance and Medicare benefits. Pricing is based on a series of multiple transactions in a drug supply chain, which includes manufacturers, wholesalers, pharmacies, providers, PBMs, and patients (Hernandez & Hung, 2024). If the reimbursement rates for healthcare services and procedures are established for Medicare, which in turn are used as a baseline rate for private insurance and Medicaid, why not pharmaceuticals?

With pharmaceutical companies taking 9 to 11 percent of every healthcare dollar, we sure spend a lot of time and attention wrestling with costs and consumer/patient burdens. Is the HIC free market business mentality operating outside of the healthcare system here? And why outside of the healthcare system when pharmaceuticals are critical for treatment plans? Power, control, and money. Systems thinking across the healthcare system between the HIC, the payers, the providers, the policymakers, and the consumers/patients is needed here. Connections, communication, and willingness among the parties involved are needed to test new models.

Understanding the sectors as part of an integrated US healthcare system is critical for successful change. Because change in one part of the system is never isolated and will ultimately reach and affect the other system sectors, systems thinking is essential to ensure that any change plan is successful and sustainable.

When the Sectors Do Work Together

Sustainable healthcare programs are essential to supporting the health needs of any population. Supporting these needs requires intentional connections between the sectors and deliberate relationship-building to consider issues through the lens of each sector. Initiating and sustaining change happens when the sectors think ahead and plan the impact of any innovation on all the other healthcare sectors. When systems thinking is working, the effect is powerful. Let's look at the ways that it is working.

CLINICAL PRACTICE CHANGE: PATIENTS, PAYERS, PROVIDERS, AND POLICYMAKERS

Return to the example of the preterm birth prevention program, where grant funding ran out for six clinics, leaving no money in the budget to pay for additional staffing. How was the funding issue overcome? We used a systems thinking approach with all the sectors at the table to keep this program viable.

A meeting was called to bring together the members of the citywide board who had worked to solicit the grants in the first place.

These leaders had come together to support the national grants, as the high infant mortality rate was a major concern across the city. They represented corporations located in the city, community leader advocates, city health department providers, and providers working on the project. However, while this was a strong mix of representatives from the community and the providers sector, there were no payers.

With the threat of no money to keep the program going, these leaders came back to the table to address the problem and discuss how to work with Medicaid (a statewide payer) to fund the new model of care in the city. Additional members were invited to the board, comprising policy sector representatives, including the state health director and a city legislator, to gain access and influence with the Medicaid program.

It took two years, and with research-based data collected for one of the national grantors to show the program results, along with documentation from the providers, consumers/patients, and policymakers, we demonstrated success related to each of these sectors' purposes.

In the end, Medicaid agreed to pay for the service. With Medicaid funding in place, the preterm birth prevention program targeting that group of low-income, at-risk pregnant moms was established permanently. Interestingly, following the acceptance of Medicaid as the funding source, a major private payer in the city also introduced the program to city obstetricians and said they would pay for this prevention care for pregnant mothers who had their insurance and were at risk of preterm labor. The program model's success was also presented at both healthcare payer and healthcare provider national conferences.

MANAGING GOVERNMENT PROGRAMS: POLICY, PAYERS, HEALTH INDUSTRIAL COMPLEX, AND PROVIDERS

While we consider the government directly involved in the health-care system, much of the work is conducted through public–private partnerships (PPPs). These PPP entities are long-term contracts between government agencies and private parties, providing a public asset or service in which the private party bears significant risk and management responsibility (World Bank Group, 2015). A PPP relies on recognizing and accepting that the government and private businesses each have certain advantages relative to the other in performing specific tasks.

The responsibilities of a private business might entail finance, design, construction, operations, management, and maintenance of a project, while the government provides planning, assessment, regulatory support, and funding. PPPs can be a tool to increase access to more quality infrastructure services for more people. When designed well and implemented in a balanced regulatory environment, PPPs can bring greater efficiency and sustainability to the provision of public services. Healthcare system PPPs result from working from the star's center and are made possible through systems thinking involving the appropriate sectors to achieve program sustainability.

In the US, there are several well-known examples of health system PPPs, such as the Medicare Advantage program, where the government pays for the care and the partner manages the money and the care. As you read in the payers sector chapter, with traditional Medicare, the government directly pays the providers for healthcare services.

Unlike traditional Medicare, the Medicare Advantage program is a PPP. Here, the government contracts with a private insurer and provides Medicare funds to the insurer, which bears the financial risk and manages the money through its operations management and quality oversight, including payments to the providers.

The providers offer additional services through Medicare Advantage that traditional Medicare does not typically provide. These include an annual wellness check and a focus on safety in the home and mental health issues. Medicare Advantage is a vital program that is fiscally successful and has been shown to appeal to Medicare beneficiaries and purchasers.

Another type of PPP is Medicaid-managed care plans, where the Medicaid population is insured by a private health insurance company using Medicaid-allocated money from the government. Like Medicare Advantage, these models have proved to be cost-effective, maintaining quality of care and, at times, improving care. These PPPs add features and benefits that more rigorously protect our general welfare, unlike the bureaucracies.

Greater protection of consumer welfare includes the use of evidence-based practice (EBP) guidelines and funding for social support services. In addition, greater efficiency and sustainability have been demonstrated. Looking at the star, the arrows show the vital relationships between all the sectors: policy, payers, providers, the HIC, and consumers/patients.

VALUE-BASED PAYMENTS: PROVIDERS, PAYERS, CONSUMERS/PATIENTS, AND POLICYMAKERS

Value-based payments are a move away from fee-for-service billing (a direct provider-to-payer process where a set cost is listed for each procedure and appears on the bill) to paying for both the procedures and a bonus or penalty based on the quality-of-care outcomes. These quality-of-care outcomes, or "value-defined care" measures, include the policymakers setting the best care standard, the provider delivering the best care, and the consumers/patients receiving the best care—so they all benefit.

This value-based payment billing practice was introduced gradually in stages over a ten-year period. The payment model was initially introduced in 2008 by Medicare as the largest payer in the health system and thus a strong and influential party that could make a change. Once it was established, the private payers followed along.

While value-based payments constitute a significant change in the payment process for the providers, they were within the providers' control to manage, which no doubt helped them accept this change. In this model, payments are made with either a bonus or a penalty applied to the base pay, depending on the results. Only some items on the bill are paid this way. However, this value-based pay model has specific patient outcomes, and the providers take responsibility for and control the selected patient outcomes.

Value-based payments are a form of risk and a true multi-health-care sector phenomenon carefully designed and implemented over several years. HCPs and their facilities had to make changes to meet the value targets. Targets are established for each individual organization according to its provider type, size, and patient complexity.

This is not a national one-size-fits-all payment process. It uses data from patient outcome results submitted by the provider facilities themselves to establish each provider's target goals for the year. These target goals include specific outcomes, and the providers can look at their own results and adjust the care to meet the targets. These value-based criteria are directed at the care delivered right at the patient's bedside, not the executive suite.

Examples of value-based care include reducing hospital-acquired infections, lowering hospital readmissions for specific diagnoses, and preventing patient falls while hospitalized. In the fall example, the hospital's data set the benchmark, thus setting the bonus and penalty targets. Now, bedside caregivers have the information to determine the factors leading to the risk of falling and can subsequently take fall preventive measures before a fall occurs, not after. When the outcome numbers are good, a bonus is paid. When the outcome numbers are below the target, a penalty is applied to the reimbursement.

During the first few years of Medicare's value-based payments, HCPs and the facilities were paid bonuses for good results against their benchmark numbers. After several years of this new values-based model, penalties were added according to performance against the benchmark targets. How healthcare facilities internally manage these new models is an ongoing challenge. However, success is on the upswing, which is very encouraging for all, especially the patients (Rau, 2023).

As you may surmise, not everyone within the providers sector agrees with value-based payments. Like other data-based changes, there is always the complaint that "our patients are sicker or more complex, and we should not be penalized for the hard work we do." The Commonwealth Fund (2023, February 7) reports that many physicians still want only fee-for-service reimbursements and reject any sort of risk-based models. There is resistance, and it will continue. However, where else do we not look for and pay for quality and value?

These value-based reimbursement models have been successful because adjustments have been made within the delivery system itself, resulting in improved patient care and cost savings. Many of the change efforts have been at the bedside, and bedside caregivers would like to see a flow of bonus money come their way in terms of tuition reimbursements and extra training programs. This is an example of not only thinking across the star's healthcare sectors but also applying systems thinking within one's own sector.

At the same time, hospitals with large budgets and high salaries do not like control coming from outside their sector, and value-based payments are controversial within the providers sector. This segment of power, control, and money will remain a hot topic item. However, in order to change healthcare, we must deal with it, and it currently involves four of the five sectors (CMS.gov, 2023f).

The value-based payment program was paused during the pandemic, and several changes are being made as it is being reinstituted post-pandemic. To look up the results for a specific hospital, go to the CMS website, which lists hospitals by their CMS numbers. KFF also lists hospitals by state and hospital name.

RETAIL SITE HEALTHCARE SERVICES: HEALTH INDUSTRIAL COMPLEX, PROVIDERS, CONSUMERS/PATIENTS, AND POLICYMAKERS

While the move to retail-based care centers belongs to the HIC sector, the providers who initially did not favor these sites have become more accepting. A retail-based care center is a clinical care site located in a retail store. An example of this is a CVS MinuteClinic that offers medical and behavioral health services. Consumers and patients can take part in wellness programs and receive low-intensity acute care at convenient locations and hours in these retail-based care centers.

Two sectors, providers and the HIC, have reached out directly to consumers and patients, coming together in response to the demands (read "requests") of consumers and patients who seek convenience. As this new provider site venue has grown, policymakers have also adapted their licensing criteria to cover these sites. These retail-based care centers have expanded dramatically in some parts of the country. In other places, large hospital provider systems in competition with these privately owned retail clinics have also developed their own urgent care sites.

The Triple Aim and the Hidden Triple Aim

Working across the sectors allows us to quickly identify both the Triple Aim and the Hidden Triple Aim at play. This is where, in making changes, we can anticipate achieving the Triple Aim goals of quality of care, population health, and cost-effectiveness. However, it is also here that power, control, and money issues become apparent.

Looking at each sector, we see some challenges related to working in the sectors across the star. As the only sector solely focused on healthcare, providers should eventually be present at every discussion, whether it concerns delivering care to consumers/patients; charging for care and getting paid; using the latest drugs, medical tests, and treatments; or passing laws related to healthcare services and payments.

The providers sector is a legacy sector that doesn't make changes quickly or easily. Providers do not like referring to healthcare as a business. Providers can also hang on to things that have always been done a certain way. This sector is hierarchical and highly structured based on education and training. As a result, consumers pay more for high-risk, highly complicated healthcare. The healthcare system has a long way to go before seriously rewarding preventive and early care and chronic care management. The current model, which usually entails waiting until a consumer becomes a sick patient, can turn into expensive, dangerous care that does not always guarantee a good outcome.

However, providers have recognized the need to listen to consumers' and patients' voices. Hospitals have added patient advocate seats to their boards. With value-based payments, there has been increased coordination between institutionally based providers and outpatient care services, services provided in patients' homes, and community-based organizations.

Payers and consumers/patients talk to one another directly, and sometimes pleasantly, when the payer has a case manager who works with healthy individuals to maintain their health and even pays for health clubs and exercise programs. Other times, it is not so pleasant, such as when addressing whether a proposed or performed medical service or treatment will not or has not been paid for, or perhaps when the patient is responsible for a portion of the bill as part of a deductible or for a service that is not covered by the payer agreement. Legislators and their staff will always listen and sometimes help with a problem.

Of course, there is the media—not an arm of the star but a great influence on policymaking. Depending on the size and extent of a problem, the press will pay attention. However, recall that the healthcare system addresses individual needs, and every case can be unique. Once it makes it into the public realm, there is a concern that it will get blown out of proportion. The public and policymakers will respond to the press; however, the media is a tool to use cautiously.

Finally, the HIC has a significant direct-to-consumer (or -patient) marketing business that includes advertising for medications and self-monitoring devices for conditions such as diabetes and atrial fibrillation. In general, the HIC relates to the other sectors as a way of getting work done. It offers an excellent example of using systems thinking to work across the sectors of the star.

Summary

Systems thinking across all the healthcare sectors is critical and challenging. In a system this size, time is also a factor. Looking at the arrows between the sectors, people who think both strategically and operationally will have an advantage in pursuing work between the sectors in both the immediate and long term.

A medical care practice change made with no permanent source of payment is in danger of being no change at all. A change made by policymakers that never gets to the examining room or the bedside is another example of a change in danger of being no change at all. And as pointed out, using a systems thinking approach when working within one's own sector is oftentimes critical for making sustainable changes.

Leadership is critical, and so is communication. Having an open mind, working across sectors, and patience are the keys to success:

1. Never forget the Triple Aim. Every sector has this goal, and it is the link to initiating conversations with all the other sectors as part of the change development process.

2. When planning and executing change initiatives, it is critical to think of the five sectors and how each is potentially involved. Change initiatives should be designed with implementation steps that examine the involvement of and establish relationships with the other sectors.

3. Bringing the other sectors to the planning table adds insight and perspective to both the immediate and long-term

change processes. Communication across the system is a critical success factor.

4. Leadership structures, such as boards, planning committees, and community-based initiatives, have been demonstrated to be successful in planning and launching change initiatives in a systems thinking mode.

5. Systems thinking involves frontline staff in every sector who are supported in initiating change when leadership takes interest and invests time to listen and respond, not react. In turn, leadership benefits from listening to and working with frontline staff who have a tactical and operational perspective and can bring practicality to strategic initiatives.

CHAPTER 9
The Paramount Issues

The five sectors must cooperate to create sustainable change. Once they begin to work together, change is possible. Within our healthcare system, there are four paramount issues that must be considered when planning and implementing change. They exist in all five sectors and represent significant areas of concern. They should be part of the conversation and accounted for in every change plan initiative:

1. Population and public health

2. The high costs of healthcare and control efforts

3. Consumers versus patients

4. The introduction of AI

It is essential for the well-being of individuals and our communities that the five sectors work together in the change planning process and address these paramount issues. Leaders act from the star's center to create change by using systems thinking.

Population Health

My earliest career days were spent as a public health nurse in inner cities. Since then, I have maintained an interest in population health and the health of our communities overall. Yet I also realize that, relative to acute care, population and public health are seemingly secondary in the overall US healthcare system.

Population health is one of the Triple Aims, which means not only is it a priority, but it is also a paramount issue, because while we have worked on the Triple Aims for almost twenty years, when we look at our population health results, the picture is dismal. Our statistics tell us there is inequity in the system.

When assessed by race and ethnicity, there are poorer health status and life expectancy rates among specific population groups. With the prevalence of an acute care model, population health is less urgent. There is little power, control, and money in population health, which may sound good, but this has likely led to a Hidden Triple Aim overload on the acute care side.

Now, we must consider whether the acute care medical model may be a barrier to the population's primary care delivery modalities. Yes, individual providers are caring and committed. However, highly educated, highly trained, and highly paid providers naturally want to focus their careers on the labor-intensive work of acute care, utilizing their skill sets and earning them financial rewards.

Population health requires different expertise and has suffered in the face of this ever-increasingly sophisticated workforce. Our healthcare system must expand access to primary care for the underserved and those cared for only in an acute care model. The system needs to focus on and initiate public health preventive care. A focus on preventive care reduces the costs of care. That means more primary care, more prevention, more aggressive management of chronic illnesses, and more care delivered outside of hospitals.

Good care results in a healthy population and lower costs. So let's look at the numbers. In a recent report, *Advancing Racial Equity in US Health Care*, the Commonwealth Fund (2024) addresses health outcomes, care access, quality of care, and use of healthcare services. The report's top three findings are as follows:

1. Deep-seated racial and ethnic disparities in health status persist across the US, even in states with high-performing health systems.

2. American Indians and Black Americans die at significantly higher rates from preventable and treatable causes compared with members of other racial and ethnic groups.

3. Substantial health and healthcare disparities exist between white communities and the Black, Hispanic, and American Indian and Alaska Native (AIAN) communities in nearly all states.

Other report findings include that Black and AIAN groups are more likely to die from treatable conditions and during or after pregnancy. Their children are more likely to die in infancy in comparison with other groups. And there is a higher risk of contracting chronic health conditions. All these groups lack affordable quality healthcare and have difficulty getting timely treatments. There are higher poverty rates, where they live has higher levels of pollution and crime, and many people will delay care due to medical debt.

In a 2022 *Health Affairs* examination of structural racism, the focus turns to the design of our healthcare system (Yearby et al., 2022). The lack of equitable access stands out, and one can make an overall statement that US health policy creates structures in the system to advantage the white population. The lack of equitable access among traditionally underserved populations, such as Black and AIAN groups, as well as rural populations, was highlighted during the pandemic, as seen in the disproportionate rates of infections, death, and access to vaccines.

Interestingly, the *Health Affairs* report notes that most Americans receive healthcare through employer-sponsored insurance. In 2019, 58 percent of American workers had employer-sponsored health insurance. But when the numbers are broken down into those with coverage, 66 percent of white workers, 47 percent of Black workers, 43 percent of Latinx workers, and 37 percent of AIAN workers had coverage. Why? Because lower-paid workers are often ineligible for insurance benefit coverage, and racial and ethnic workers frequently have lower-paying positions.

So, what are we doing? These outcome numbers are not unknown, and there have been and currently are a wide variety of programs, clinical models, and community-based initiatives to address inequities and improve the overall health of our population. There are programs in place, from major healthcare provider systems to local clinics. However, as the *Health Affairs* article points out, part of the problem is both a system and health policy issue, and until the major sectors address it wholly, healthcare disparities will be hit and miss.

Let's look at two initiatives. The first major national effort was launched in July 2023 with the Joint Commission's (n.d.) "New Requirements to Reduce Health Care Disparities" in the accreditation process. Working with the National Quality Forum, the Joint Commission (2023) accreditation criteria are designed to support the national patient safety goal to improve healthcare disparities.

These accreditation criteria apply to ambulatory healthcare sites, behavioral healthcare services, healthcare and human resources, critical access hospitals, and full hospital accreditation programs. The accreditation process includes defining disparities and specific population goals, setting an improvement goal, and identifying and addressing the strategies and resources required to achieve the goal and the lessons learned. The disparity accreditation process has been introduced; however, it is too early to know the results.

The second major initiative is redesigning the value-based payment programs, a policy-generated model described in the providers sector. Introduced by Medicare and adopted by private insurance, value-based payments focus on the hospital experience. The concept of value-based payments is beneficial, as it includes outcomes concerning patient status and reporting specific measurable conditions. Targets are set using a hospital's data, and bonuses or penalties are paid based on the results. Value-based care is theoretically good for all patients, and bedside providers have worked hard to enhance care, resulting in bonus payments being made.

Unfortunately, these payment opportunities have not worked for hospitals with a high percentage of racial and ethnic diversity. The payment model focuses on outcomes and does not factor in influencers that impact a lower socioeconomic population's outcomes. Such influencers include preexisting conditions and a lack of community and social support directly aiding patients in stabilizing their health status. Both can negatively affect the outcome results on which the value-based payment models are built. With value-based targets not being met, these hospitals are frequently financially penalized, taking money away that could be used to supply other critical medical services.

The design and launch of advanced value-based payment models that address the social determinants of health and patient access to government support and specialty social support services will assist hospitals in reaching their targets and meeting the needs of the patients themselves (Hart, 2024; Horstman, 2023; Navathe & Liao, 2022). With success demonstrated in the first round of value-based payment models, it is critical that we prioritize this effort to introduce new value-based payments created to improve the health of the population. In moving care to outpatient services, there is a possibility of a reduction in revenue for those hospitals that rely heavily on inpatient services. Advanced value-based payments need to provide the opportunity to balance out these two unequal revenue sources.

Today, the critical importance of population health is enjoying a resurgence, and we are seeing the incorporation of early public health levels of care. With millions of dollars in their annual budgets, hospitals can innovate and introduce population health models. It is also critical that today's hospitals link their workforces with community-based care options and facilitate moving care out of the highest-cost setting.

Ability is one thing, but motivation is critical when considering a change from a highly intensive medical treatment center to a clinically integrated model working across the healthcare delivery system. Letting go of the legacy system is essential. In the case of not-for-profit hospitals, the tax exemption is not directly tied to the community benefits.

The Affordable Care Act (ACA) contains a community donation clause for hospitals; however, it is not clearly defined or assessed on a regular basis. In a study conducted by the Lown Institute for the US House of Representatives in April 2023 on tax-exempt hospitals and this community-based standard, referred to as community giveback, the hospital community giveback was highly variable and ran the gamut of significant to insignificant (Garber, 2023). Mega-system hospitals must address population health adequately and maintain traditional high-level care capabilities.

With public and private insurance value-based payments, community-based primary care is receiving more attention as these insurance models reward prevention and early intervention. If the illness can be prevented in the first place, waiting until a patient requires intensive-level acute care makes no sense. As the American Heart Association describes it, our healthcare system focus should be on "upstream prevention and chronic care treatments" to avoid "downstream high-cost interventions" (Warner et al., 2020).

The time has come for a new model and framework focused on primary care and emphasizing health equity through evidence-based quality care, safety, efficiency, and satisfaction, both for the consumer/patient and the healthcare provider.

By shifting the focus to systems thinking and looking at the whole from the star's center, we can effectively address these pressing issues in our country. It's not just an economic imperative but also a beacon of hope. Too many of our vital social support programs rely solely on grants. We must embrace hard dollars and innovative financial models that don't compromise clinical services.

The High Costs of Care and Control Efforts

One of the most contentious areas in today's health system is the high cost of care. It is a constant and consistent message and likely the single biggest driver for change advocates. When sitting in the examining room, the health system's $4.9 trillion money flow is difficult to fathom. Yet the overall cost of care in a system this size is built piece by piece, including the cost of the care given and received in that examining room. These costs place the health system as the second-largest industry in the US. These costs will continue to rise, reaching a projected $6+ trillion annual spend by 2030 (CMS.gov, 2022).

The rising care costs can influence you daily, whether you are insured by a private payer and facing deductibles, increased premiums, co-pays, or coinsurance or are a Social Security beneficiary with a significant Medicare benefit deduction from your monthly check. Or perhaps you are an employer struggling to offer health insurance as an employee benefit. All these money-related concerns result from the rising costs of healthcare.

In the previous chapters, there are descriptions of the rise in medical inflation beginning in the 1970s and 1980s and the resulting numerous control factors, such as managed care, case management, utilization reviews, provider networks, and contracts between payers and providers. As a result of these efforts, the rate of medical inflation decreased, which tells us that change efforts are possible and can work.

However, in the late 2000s, medical inflation began to rise again. Was it a result of the ACA and the success in reducing the number of uninsured people, thereby bringing more people into the system and resulting in growth in the overall system? And if so, was the growth uncontrollable? It's possible.

The top items identified as contributing to the high care costs are numerous. These include costly medical procedures, rising drug prices, and an emphasis on acute care, leading to overtreatment and unnecessary procedures. Add waste and fragmented care with a lack of coordination between providers. Administrative complexity, the lack of price transparency, hidden fees, and an overemphasis on profits lead to overutilization and unnecessary procedures.

The recent trend of private equity investment in physician practices and hospital systems has now emphasized creating earnings for investors, which must be paid and can potentially impact the bottom line. The expansion of major hospital systems has not reduced costs as promised. With the acquisition of more and more physician practices by hospital systems, hospital administrative charges are now being added to outpatient service bills (Evans, 2024).

In terms of changes to the healthcare models, there are concerns with medical errors, inconsistent treatments, forgoing prevention and primary care, and denying the wishes of the dying, as well as introducing new technologies and treatments that are not more effective than the ones currently used. These are significant drivers of high costs and are major concerns.

With these listed in one place, they appear overwhelming. At the same time, all five sectors are continuously putting efforts in place to control the costs. The previous chapters on each sector describe these efforts. However, these efforts are frequently considered one-sided power and control efforts implemented in one or two sectors.

As the other sectors become involved, cost controls may fail because not all sectors have been fully considered during the cost-control design phase. For example, consider managed care, an arrow intersection between payers and providers. Once the policy sector got involved, things began to get out of control. In some managed care models, the risk pool was originally the provider's responsibility to manage, with the intention of better money management.

However, this was not always successful, and if the money included government funds, government bureaucrats acted and moved the risk pools back to the insurer, resulting in additional levels of oversight from the insurance company, which the providers found intrusive and time-consuming. And the original intent—to keep the providers connected to the reality of the care costs—was transferred back to the payers.

This brings us to another question related to the care costs and the prices paid. If government entitlement programs are the lowest payers, and the costs associated with these services are shifted to private payers who make up the difference by paying a higher price for the same care, is there a difference in the quality of care between the two payment sources? Unlike purchasing a consumer good, where a different price reflects the product's quality, we cannot ethically provide a model of care with differences based on the prices paid.

The care should theoretically be the same regardless of the amount paid. So, is this shifting of costs from public payers to private payers keeping the costs and prices high because everyone is getting what they want: patients are receiving care, providers are getting the money they want and need, and payers have contracts with providers that keep the providers in the payer's participating provider network?

Another reason why we have high costs is waste and overutilization. Often used together to describe the problem, waste and overutilization are separate. Waste is unnecessary care, costly diagnostics, or treatments that are not necessarily needed. An example is using a surgical treatment before trying physical therapy.

Overutilization is often duplicative diagnostics and treatment, sometimes the only choice when a patient record is unattainable—something that is not rare. With the move to EHRs and the privacy walls protecting patient information, providers often repeat tests, treatments, and therapies because they're blind to the previous procedures and care. Incomplete and inadequate information is a big problem, as is communication between patients and their providers.

Then there is evidence-based practice (EBP). It seems simple for payers to state that research-based and tested treatment guidelines should be implemented and followed everywhere. That is the basis of utilization management conducted by the payers. But get inside that examining room and try telling the provider and patient to follow a recipe card. Remember the default provider comment: "The insurance company is making me do this."

Most of us want to believe that every patient is different and unique, and the treatment model is designed with this in mind. This just isn't always so. One wonders whether the introduction of AI can address this lack of following evidence-based treatment models. We shall see.

What happens when a patient asks for an alternative treatment model? If you are a provider and have studied, practiced, and specialized in a particular treatment model, why wouldn't that be the choice? Consumers and patients need to assume that there may be treatment options. They need to ask questions and take part in the decision-making process.

If the consumer or patient remains uncertain, there is always an option to get a second opinion, which some patients choose. Others, fearing that they are insulting their primary provider or the specialist, will stay with the first treatment option and not pursue alternatives. It would be fascinating to hear a provider say to a patient, "You may want to get a second opinion before we proceed with this treatment."

It is common knowledge that lifestyle and general health status influence treatment options. With the focus turned to the disparities in health outcomes and the identification of marked differences in the connection between patient socioeconomic and health status, socioeconomics is now being looked at and addressed in population health initiatives. These are important and must be standardized and paid for (CMS.gov, n.d.-a; Radley et al., 2024). For better or worse, we—and that means every one of us—need to address the high cost of care, the waste, the overutilization, and our role in taking care of ourselves.

Over the decades, private corporations have entered the arena, bringing innovative think tanks and financial backing. They have introduced new models of managing costs and care. An example is Kaiser Permanente, which sought to create its own pay and provider organization, focusing on quality of care and stepping away from the more traditional insurance and health provider systems.

Costs are managed by reducing overtreatment, moving upstream to less acute care and earlier treatment interventions, and transparent pricing with reasonable costs. With the 2023 launch of a Kaiser subsidiary, Risant Health, there is now an effort to unite other systems, such as Geisinger Health, into a group organization of like-minded, nonprofit, value-oriented, and community-based healthcare systems and to make this available around the US.

Another example of an innovative nonprofit organizational launch was the creation of Haven Healthcare by Amazon, Berkshire Hathaway, and JPMorgan Chase in 2018. With the 1.2 million employees of these three companies, there was an assumption that this would be a large enough population to work with and make changes. However, the employees were spread across the country, and Haven could not gain market power or price concessions from the providers. The providers did not make it easy, preferring to keep healthcare services focused on the existing models. What Haven failed to do from the start was to work with the providers to build the company. It was not systems thinking among the sectors of the star, and this resulted in the closure of Haven (Toussaint, 2021).

Medical debt remains a concern and can result in significant problems for consumers, patients, payers, and providers. Legal assistance is available through some consumer groups, as well as local legal aid entities.

Healthcare is not all science. We are dealing with human beings and an industry. And we must address the high costs. The health industry's world rankings, alongside poor population health outcomes, tell us that even though we spend a lot of money, there is room for improvement. With many concerns and causes related to the high costs, we cannot simply throw more money at the problem, thinking there will be a solution. Change agents must employ systems thinking and work with all sectors. And long-range strategic planning is critical.

There is no solution until these issues are resolved across the star.

Consumers Versus Patients

Most people can be considered healthcare consumers, and they hope to spend little time as patients requiring acute care. A consumer model of care is less costly and can significantly reduce the rising costs of patient care. However, shifting from patient-centric healthcare to a consumer model has resulted in a significant cultural change.

This is significant because, with a consumer model, the hundred-year-old acute care model focusing on patients and treating sickness is redirected to considerably more people, while a new primary care model focuses on prevention and maintenance for most of the population. This model requires consumers to change their perspective and use the system differently from how they did in the past. The consumer healthcare model has three components:

1. Self-care and responsibility to manage one's health status on the part of consumers and patients alike

2. Changes in the healthcare delivery model, with a broadened focus on prevention and chronic illness management

3. Price transparency to address high costs and provide critical information to consumers and patients in managing their use of the healthcare system

It is important to point out that there is a consumer model of healthcare; however, the overall focus of the healthcare system remains on acute care and the technology of our present-day health system. Additionally, with a consumer model of care, the providers, payers, and policymakers sectors need to come together and make changes focused on new models of care. The HIC is already there.

With this consumer model of healthcare, consumers themselves need to take responsibility for their own health and well-being, beginning with diet, exercise, and wellness. Understanding self-care and health maintenance is very much a part of the consumer model. We also need direction and guidance from our healthcare provider teams to change our lifestyles and improve our state of wellness.

Everyone needs access to care in a new consumer-model health system. While 20 percent of physicians work in primary care, the majority of the others remain focused on costly tertiary treatment models—that is, treatment delivered after a problem has reached an acute care point. It will take time to change the direction of this primary care model, but it is critical for our population and the healthcare system to do so.

Consumer access to other provider specialties is often limited, as physicians manage the referral process. Physicians are the gate to primary care nurse practitioners, nurse-midwives, physician assistants, social workers, and other therapists. And this gate needs to be opened. Policymakers also need to open practice gates instead of using legislation to stifle practice by non-physicians. A "provider mix" combines a variety of specialty providers who address the population's needs.

This is a sound alternative for consumers with primary and chronic care needs. Not every healthcare service needs to be managed by a physician. We need to add social support services to primary and chronic care management to educate consumers better and help maintain their state of health.

Medical homes and Accountable Care Organizations (ACOs) are strong models that emphasize primary and chronic care. Yet they need to grow and expand to add aggressive preventive care models to the provider options when giving care. They have not been launched in the numbers anticipated to meet the population's needs.

In a consumer model, providers must introduce self-monitoring technology into their practice and partner with consumers to use it to manage their care. Consumers and patients are already purchasing and using these monitors, wristbands, and phone apps to provide data on their health status. These data can be a more significant part of care management when consumers work with their providers to maximize the benefit of the technology.

For the payers, a consumer model of care is new, and with its focus on preventive care, it will impact the sector that currently pays for care when a treatment is delivered. Payers will need to pay for preventive and chronic care services, as well as social support actions. How will we model payments for prevention? How will the sectors work together to design this? All this needs to happen.

The new value-based care payment models (described in the payers and providers sector chapters) are a good start because they have changed the model of care with a focus on consumer and patient outcomes and bonus money to providers. Recommendations are now being given to expand the value payment models relative to health equity and outcomes. Policymakers, as well as private payers, can and will want to further these changes.

Price transparency is a key item on the consumer list, and it's a concept that payers, providers, and policymakers are required to introduce. But what does it entail? According to CMS, price transparency is the provision of readily available information on the cost of healthcare services. This is aimed at enabling patients and other purchasers to identify, compare, and choose providers that offer a desired level of value (CMS.gov, 2023b).

Since January 1, 2021, with the introduction of several federal acts, such as the Hospital Price Transparency rule, the Transparency in Coverage final rules, and the No Surprises Act, hospitals have been mandated to disclose their standard charges. These include the rates they negotiate with insurance companies and the discounted prices they are willing to accept from a patient if paid in cash. This information is meant to be publicly available, but its accessibility is currently a challenge (American Hospital Association, 2023a).

According to Mathematics.org, these price transparency requirements are available to help patients avoid unexpected medical bills and better manage their healthcare expenses. They also increase the accountability of the providers, who should be posting fair and competitive prices. These are positives for the price transparency model. However, the American Hospital Association (2023a) blatantly writes that the process is not always easy to implement and track. In addition, it requires a degree of complexity and cost to implement and keep up to date.

On July 1, 2022, the federal requirements were extended to most group health plans and issuers of group or individual health insurance, which began posting information on covered items and services. On January 1, 2023, and January 1, 2024, CMS issued two additional requirements on the kind of information that needs to be posted by these payers. Price transparency is a complex undertaking and takes time to implement.

Price transparency is here, and if it becomes a practical reality and consumers genuinely understand how it works and how they can use it, price transparency will be a form of consumerism. But first, the information must be usable, and then consumers will need to learn what to do with the information. This will take time. The consumer/patient responsibilities for deductibles, co-pays, and coinsurance and the concept of in- and out-of-network providers are all frustrating. Medical debt is a problem. And yes, consumers are paying for government care with their tax dollars. (The payers chapter describes the cost shift in more detail.) Everyone needs to know what this means in terms of their wallets.

Consumers will need to work with providers to seek alternative treatment plans and actively engage in managing the delivery and use of their healthcare services. This is the strength of this sector, and it is an area of tremendous possibility. For the consumers, all of these initiatives are designed as benefits. The intent is to lower costs and improve outcomes and our health status. However, like everything else, we will have to work at this to get results.

The Introduction of Artificial Intelligence

In the nation's second-largest industry, AI will undoubtedly be introduced and utilized throughout the five sectors. AI is now everywhere, yet healthcare has traditionally been slow to adopt significant changes. From ethical considerations to patient safety and responsible utilization, AI integration is a multifaceted undertaking for our industry. As a tool in the delivery of healthcare services, it is important to ensure that we know when AI is being used and that AI is not making decisions without human oversight. AI can support clinical decision-making and be a part of the process of delivering healthcare.

So where is the potential? The ultimate prize is to enhance and ensure safe, effective, and evidence-based healthcare delivery to the population. AI has great potential, requiring commitment and involvement across all five sectors, beginning at the bench and continuing to the bedside. AI can support and augment the humans in the industry, but we humans must always remain in control.

There are two AI categories: predictive AI, which analyzes data to make a prediction, and generative AI, which produces new content based on or built off existing data. AI can be applied in four major areas: basic science and research, clinical practice, operational streamlining, and the potential for enhancing patient engagement and satisfaction—essentially all five sectors of the health system.

Predictive AI models and machine learning have existed for almost a decade. Generative AI can summarize medical records and automate clinical note-taking. However, the early generative AI models are not yet complete enough to guarantee the technology's accuracy, performance, and safety (Landi, 2024).

In an AI seminar hosted by Duke AI Health, Michael Pencina, who spearheaded Duke University's role as the founding partner of the Coalition for Health AI (https://www.coalitionforhealthai.org/) and who is an internationally recognized authority on the evaluation of AI tools and algorithms (Duke University School of Medicine, 2024), laid out four principles for the responsible use of AI by the healthcare industry:

1. Ensure AI technology serves humans

2. Define the tasks we want AI to accomplish

3. Describe what successful use of AI tools looks like

4. Create transparent systems for continuously testing and monitoring AI tools

The goals of these principles are the following:

1. Keep the focus on patient safety and quality of care

2. Enhance patient satisfaction

3. Streamline operations and address physician and nursing burnout

While major AI initiatives are underway, we must ensure that implementation has oversight from health system leaders who bring order, rigor, and discipline to developing and implementing AI in clinical practice. In an editorial in *NEJM AI*, Kohane (2023) writes about the crucial need for AI in medicine to undergo the same level of scrutiny as any clinical intervention. If the implementation goal is to improve patient care, we are reminded that we must bear a constant awareness that the misuse or careless implementation of these technologies without rigorous oversight or assessment may precipitate systemic harm to all parties in the healthcare system—most importantly, the patients.

The following includes key areas where AI products are being developed or used within the five sectors.

HEALTH INDUSTRIAL COMPLEX

As already noted in this book, a significant amount of health system research is conducted within the HIC sector. It is essential for this sector to establish a disciplined and transparent process for developing and testing AI. This transparent process, once established, can serve as a model for others to follow.

Like other healthcare system initiatives, the immediate focus should be on conducting pilot studies to test the efficiency of all AI products before rolling them out carte blanche (Kohane, 2023).

Piloting an AI initiative is critical in ensuring the effectiveness and efficiency of AI products under development. Furthermore, additional rigorous study and assessment are necessary to fully integrate and accept the introduction of AI into patient care. In the rush to adopt AI, it is vital not to overlook these steps in the planning and design of AI tools, as well as in the introduction and execution of AI-supported models.

Close examination and assessment, or research, if necessary, must also be developed to track and validate the standards and practices that AI recommends—that is, testing and validating that the proposed AI models meet the needs of specific patient populations and service models. This validation should occur through small pilots to monitor the implementation of an AI system over time.

The aim of the validation is to evaluate what is happening in real time with AI technology. Validation must include reviewing the patients and the healthcare organizations using AI technology. A single AI model may not be specific to the needs of particular populations and providers. Why? Because populations and providers can be different, and there is no one-size-fits-all model for the delivery of healthcare.

Further, racial bias is a significant concern, and with a reliance on current practices and the findings noted in the population paramount issue, AI, unfortunately, can continue these biases. In her book *Unmasking AI*, Buolamwini (2023) describes the bias built into contemporary computerized tech products. She calls for algorithmic justice coupled with civil rights to address this looming and potentially harmful situation.

The numbers in the population's health are a paramount issue that must motivate us to change. Indeed, the focus should be on the tech world as a top priority and a critical place for problem-solving.

Again, look back at the four principles for the responsible use of AI: serving humans, defining what AI must accomplish, describing what successful use of AI tools looks like, and creating transparent systems for continuously testing and monitoring AI tools.

In my reading and other discoveries on this AI topic, I have yet to encounter the following concern centered on an HIC sector issue that profoundly impacts AI. In his book *Code Blue*, Magee (2019, p. 230) writes, "Bottom line, the American system of research is rife with unethical conduct and financial conflict of interest." He tells us that US companies sponsor research in other countries with less strict research guidelines, so how can we be sure about a study's rigor or the reliability of its results?

On the surface, this underscores the urgent need for stricter guidelines and transparency in research sponsorship, and it also affects the downstream effects on AI, which will be less than complete in its information gathering and assessment. With researchers less likely to publish poor results, known as publication bias, AI will be incomplete in its information gathering and assessment. This not only highlights the need for transparency and accountability but also the effect that this will have on AI.

So, how does this impact AI? The learning process of an AI algorithm will be impacted if medical research mistakes and imperfect findings are never published. Think of the consequences if AI brings together all the research but needs to include research that did not work. We must ask whether the AI results are accurate and dependable. Is missing data in the AI algorithms another form of research bias? Does this become a significant threat to using AI when there is a potential dependency on this technology?

PROVIDERS

Introducing AI into healthcare practice is a change management moment. There is often a significant mismatch between the HIC's scientific development and clinicians in practice. Preparing the healthcare provider workforce to understand and use AI must ultimately ensure that the workforce feels empowered and equipped.

Data scientists must work closely with and become part of the healthcare delivery team. Nursing will be critical in this inter-sector collaboration, with their proximity to patients. Executing a change management process, alongside training and professional development for clinicians, will be necessary.

The legal issues surrounding the use of AI in healthcare are another area to watch. In his article *Medical Malpractice in the Age of AI,* Pearl (2024), referring to generative AI, asks who will bear the blame for poor outcomes, mistreatment, and malpractice—especially when AI is directly involved in consumer and patient care.

Suppose AI is providing treatment advice, for example, and directing a patient on an insulin dosage based on the blood sugar level measured by the patient. In this case, the FDA must approve this treatment algorithm. However, the FDA approves medical treatments, and not all AI is within the scope of the FDA.

PAYERS AND PROVIDERS

Billing for using AI is another area to be considered. Treatment modalities developed and delivered by AI will need to be billed. Before this becomes practice, however, Pencina's principles need to be applied.

That is, we must know how the AI process directly serves the patient and, most importantly, confirm that the AI task is well defined and rigorously tested, ensuring that the system is transparent in the specific use of AI for a specific patient. And how do providers bill for their use of AI? As Abramoff and colleagues (2024) note, a connection to the treatment will be expected.

POLICYMAKERS AND BUREAUCRACIES

Policymakers and bureaucrats are moving along with the AI oversight processes. The US Department of Health and Human Services (HHS) has an office for health information technology, established in 2004. This office supports the adoption of health informatics technology and promotes nationwide standards to improve healthcare. Regarding AI, HHS has created a national health AI pledge that healthcare systems and payers voluntarily commit to.

A federal advisory panel, the Artificial Intelligence Safety and Security Board, has been organized to protect the economy, public health, and vital industries from AI-powered threats. The board's first meeting was held in May 2024, and anticipated quarterly meetings will follow. The board members include top technology industry leaders who aim to oversee powerful AI systems (Voltz, 2024).

There is a director of the FDA's Digital Health Center of Excellence. However, the FDA cannot test and approve every algorithm because there are thousands of algorithms, and the number is growing constantly. This challenge is significant, and as of now, it is unclear how the algorithms will be monitored and approved. The FDA tests treatment modes for actual use at the bedside.

Starting in 2019, the FDA published a series of six discussion papers. These papers include guiding principles for machine learning practice for medical device development. AI does not fall under the FDA's medical device regulations, with the FDA stating that its "traditional paradigm of medical device regulation is not designed for adaptive artificial intelligence and machine learning technologies." In March 2024, a paper was jointly published by the FDA's Center for Biologics Evaluation (CBER), Center for Drug Evaluation and Research (CDER), Center for Devices and Radiological Health (CDRH), and Office of Combination Products (OCP). The paper calls for a premarket review and an overall FDA action plan to cover the potential for the exciting onslaught of AI products in the medical field. The complexity of this massive subject is seen simply in the title of the paper: *Artificial Intelligence and Medical Products: How CBER, CDER, CDRH, and OCP Are Working Together* (FDA, 2024).

ARTIFICIAL INTELLIGENCE

AI will continue to evolve as the healthcare industry leans into the efficiencies and precision it can bring to patient care and consumer health. Remembering Pencina's principles, the considerations for all healthcare sectors are that the AI tasks developed serve humans and that the systems continuously test and monitor the rigor and functionality of AI tools.

The introduction of all AI technology must focus on patient safety, satisfaction, and quality of care. The development and introduction of AI require systems thinking across the healthcare sectors to fully realize the use of AI in safe, effective, and evidence-based healthcare delivery to the population.

Summary

Each of the four paramount issues shows up in all five sectors. They are as much about the arrows between the sectors as within the sectors themselves. And here is where disruption and conflict can arise. Systems thinking allows us to see within the sector relationships where these conflicts may exist and the reasons why.

The hot topic areas, when presented by the media and often-times the policymakers, also address the four paramount issues. However, when addressed, a system-wide solution is rarely offered, and too often, it is a situation of highlighting a problem with too simple a solution offered that rests on one sector:

1. Population health concerns inequitable health status based on race and ethnicity and access to care challenges, both in terms of provider availability and the lack of payment sources. Both of these are major concerns.

2. The high costs of care are attributable to a variety of causes and include understanding and addressing:

    ★   an acute care model with rising treatment costs;
    ★   waste and overutilization;
    ★   administrative and provider financing payment models;
    ★   management of insurance risk pool monies;
    ★   varieties of treatment, ranging from lower cost to higher cost options; and
    ★   isolated efforts in one or two of the star sectors alone.

The shifting of costs from public payers to private payers may, in fact, be a win for patients, providers, payers, and policymakers. However, because of the complexity of the payer system, consumers/patients suffer financially without directly understanding why.

3. A consumer model of care has two major directions. One direction is a move from the acute care model to more primary care and long-term management of chronic illness. Here, consumer/patient responsibilities expand and are a significant part of the model's success.

The second direction concerns lowering costs and paying for care. Value-based care models focusing on outcomes and price transparency are significant, with several federal requirements passed in 2022, 2023, and 2024.

4. The introduction of AI into the US health system is a multifaceted undertaking. Ethical considerations, patient safety, and responsible utilization head the list of critical success factors. Both predictive and generative AI categories have utility across all five sectors.

R&D in the utilization of AI is underway, and major health system leadership across the five sectors currently devotes significant oversight, policymaking, and control factors to this new science. In our major health system, it is critical that we move carefully to embrace AI, knowing that its outward appeal of saving time and resources is important.

CONCLUSION

Create Change

While essential, the US healthcare system has flaws. Change is necessary, and it's up to all of us, from leaders to concerned citizens, to make it happen. By recognizing the need for change and committing to understanding the system's structure, we can drive sustainable change in the US healthcare system.

This book describes the structure and workings of the US healthcare system. It also introduces a systems thinking model that acknowledges the structure and workings of this highly complex system and argues that sustainable change is possible by considering the system as a whole rather than just its parts.

The star framework identifies each of the five sectors and their interrelationships. Systems thinking is at the star's center and requires an open mind and hard work. Communication is essential for those working to make changes across the sectors. Looking at the overall healthcare system is a good start.

Nevertheless, achieving sustainable change depends on understanding and accepting the contributions of each of the US healthcare system's five sectors, what they do, and how they are interrelated. Moreover, effective change can begin once the interrelatedness of these individual parts is considered. Conflict resolution is also a factor to be considered in many situations. Central to all change is the Triple Aim, which ensures quality and safe care, population health, and cost-effectiveness. Just as central to effective and sustainable change is understanding that there is a Hidden Triple Aim: power, control, and money.

At the top of the star framework is the healthcare system's essence: the consumers/patients sector, encompassing over 339 million people, for whom the system is designed. Taken en masse, when we look at the health of the population, we continue to see significant gaps and inequities, which, since the COVID-19 pandemic, have again gained greater attention with an intent to improve the health status of racial and ethnic groups.

Change in this sector, when possible, can be at the individual level through making lifestyle adjustments to improve health, improving access to care through telehealth, making it possible to consult with a provider outside of regular business hours, and providing additional educational awareness through public communications, including using the media and online healthcare publicity. It would not be that difficult to post a health hint of the day that pops up when we turn on our phones, televisions, or radios, and it would be an excellent reminder to take care of ourselves.

Other changes are beyond any one individual's control and include societal systemic issues requiring change leaders' attention to improve access to care in service delivery and financing healthcare, both of which are pivotal to making changes in the consumers/patients sector.

Most money flowing through the US healthcare system comes from the consumers/patients sector and goes to the payers. And while it may sound simple as written, it is a highly complex and complicated set of processes. This financing pays for the delivery of healthcare services and comes from both public and private payers. Significant differences exist in this sector's public and private payer operational models. Whether the payer is public or private, the money flow here is a significant component of the total dollar amounts, which makes the US healthcare system the second-largest industry in the US. Looking at the arrows that show the money flow between the consumers/patients, the payers, and the providers, we see $4.9 trillion in spending.

This money flow takes us to the providers sector, which is also very complex, with its endless care delivery models. This sector is powerful. However, as the source of healthcare delivery, the responsibility to make sustainable changes rests in the providers sector. The four paramount issues—population racial and ethnic disparities, rising costs and medical inflation, transitioning to a consumer model of care, and safe and effective use of AI—are all significant challenges for the providers sector. Nevertheless, by working with the other sectors, there are opportunities to innovate and significantly change the overall system.

While integral to healthcare, the health industrial complex (HIC) stands alone with its business model. Big Pharma resides in this sector and controls US medication research, development, and distribution. Big data controls medical information collection, analysis, and distribution. We must admit that some efficiencies come with being big, and the HIC's technological contributions to the overall system have been remarkable. The HIC mainly comprises for-profit businesses, from joint venture start-ups to publicly traded corporations. It supports healthcare systems worldwide.

When we think about policymakers, their role is to protect the public. Policymakers include state and federal legislators, bureaucracies, and judiciaries. Notably, this sector oversees provider licensing. It also oversees the financing of healthcare services, including the essential passage of Medicare and Medicaid in 1965. Today, the government contributes almost half of US healthcare spending annually. With taxpayers supporting the funding, the money can seem never-ending; however, it is not.

I have seen changes across the star's sectors despite the conflicts—changes that include interactions between each of the five sectors, resulting in cost-effective, high-quality, and safe care that serves large and diverse groups of consumers and patients.

Did these efforts take place overnight? No. Was there extensive planning, assessment, and replanning over several years? Yes. Who sat around the table? Policymakers, healthcare providers, payers, community-based patient representatives, advocacy groups, and administrators. Ultimately, we made a difference in people's lives. And that was not just for the patients and their families. It was a positive change in our community.

Perhaps the most significant impact of our collaborative efforts was on the individuals representing the five sectors around the table. We evolved and learned to listen, compromise, and work together, fostering a spirit of unity and understanding.

Future Casting

The following are thoughts and opinions on what hospitals and healthcare may look like in ten years, as expressed by twenty US hospital CEOs in 2022 (Muhammad, 2023). Their observations reflect how the healthcare system would look if sustainable change occurred. Not surprisingly, sustainable change includes improving the four paramount issues highlighted in this book: population health, medical cost reductions, the introduction of a consumer model of care, and the controlled and strategic introduction of AI. They highlight these ideas:

★ Overall, a healthier healthcare system will prevail if we can provide a wider spectrum of care in broader settings focused on quality and convenience.

★ The rational control of utilization across the system will be more critical than ever.

★ The hospital system itself will change as procedures become less invasive and faster.

★ Specialty hospitals will provide services regionally instead of specialty services being available in local community hospitals.

★ Local community hospitals will be the navigators to the specialty sites. (From my perspective, this might look like today's rural critical access care hospital model in some way.)

★ Telemedicine, AI, robotics, precision medicine, and smart devices will further enhance and influence how care is delivered.

★ Physicians and nurses will need training in a new healthcare model. (I suggest administrators as well, or simply all of us, will need training in a new healthcare model.)

The CEOs in this article continue to elaborate: Operationally, hospitals and healthcare systems will be designed more around the patient experience rather than the patient accommodating the hospital design and operations. Hospital design and operations include a system that is geared toward patient choice, allowing patients to shop for services, and there is price competition for out-of-pocket expenses.

To bring costs down, rational utilization control will be more critical than ever. The CEOs acknowledge that hopefully, the administrative costs of delivering care will shrink, and healthcare efficiencies will be harnessed to reduce time waste. Structurally, more care will continue to be done ambulatorily, with hospitals having significantly more beds with critical care capabilities and single rooms for infection control, putting pressure on the cost per square foot to operate. And finally, sustainable funding strategies for safety net hospitals will be needed.

When we examine the overall healthcare system, the CEOs identify a strong desire and commitment to alleviating health equity barriers and reducing fragmented care for underserved populations. The increasing presence of the social determinants of health underscores a comprehensive approach as the CDC and the World Health Organization now focus on addressing this issue.

Ultimately, we all share responsibility for addressing health equity barriers and fragmented care. This is especially true for the leaders in any of the five sectors of the healthcare system. It's our collective responsibility to communicate and support each other in this crucial work.

The Call to Action

The status quo is unacceptable. Legitimate change is necessary. So stop reacting, start acting, and get involved now. Catalyze change by initiating and leading conversations that include systems thinking and leaders in other sectors. Educate yourself on the issues by using credible information. Keep the Triple Aim out front, and never forget the Hidden Triple Aim.

Not sure where to start? Start here:

★ Prioritize the paramount issues and bring them up at every opportunity.

★ Adopt consumerism and patient choice. Launch more convenient ways to access high-quality care.

★ Alleviate equity barriers, reduce fragmented care, and factor in the social determinants of health using data.

★ Reduce waste and overutilization.

★ Watch AI and assess the proposed adoptions.

★ Request AI product study results and ask researchers how the results are validated to meet the needs of your specific patient care models.

★ Understand the legal components of all healthcare delivery systems and technologies.

★ Prioritize working with frontline caregivers.

Above all, be patient. Changing a system this size takes years. There will be numerous and varied challenges. However, always keep in mind that the US healthcare system is a system that is already constantly changing. So why not initiate effective and sustainable change through systems thinking and collaborating with others across all sectors? Now is the time to take the lead and keep going!

APPENDIX
Finding Trustworthy Information

Janene Batten, EdD

In the digital age, finding information has become a breeze, empowering you with a wealth of knowledge at your fingertips. However, discerning its trustworthiness is a different challenge altogether.

Information trustworthiness is crucial for decision-making and user confidence. Consuming wrong or fake information leads to severe consequences, including the proliferation of ever-increasing circles of misinformation. Misinformation is the unintentional sharing of false, inaccurate, or incomplete information, whereas disinformation is the intentional spread of false information (Heiss, 2020).

Establishing credibility and trust hinges on using authoritative and reliable sources. Authoritative and reliable sources provide well-researched information based on the most current and accurate data. These sources include

★ scholarly, peer-reviewed articles and books;

★ professional and trade organization white papers, articles, and books;

★ books and newspaper and magazine articles from well-established companies; and

★ education, government, and research institute websites.

Where to start for more information on some of the topics included in this book? While not exhaustive, the references noted in each chapter include valuable examples of reliable and credible information sources. For other sources, it's important to consider these key factors when evaluating their credibility and trustworthiness:

Check the credentials:

★ Is the author an expert, or are they writing on behalf of a well-respected source, such as the Commonwealth Fund, the Kaiser Family Foundation (KFF), or the Public Interest Research Group (PIRG-Health)?

★ Does the author currently work in the field or have a long history of working in the field? Check to see whether they have a presence on LinkedIn, or do a quick Google search to find out more about their authority in the area.

Examine the URLs:

★ When evaluating website credibility, it's crucial to consider the internet domain (the URL ending). Websites with .org (a registered organization), .gov (a government agency), and .edu (an educational institution) are generally reliable and credible.

★ .com websites are often credible but may have a commercial aspect. Be sure to follow up to check the citations for any biases that lean toward a particular point of view with the intent to influence the reader (more about biases below).

★ Information from countries outside the US is an opportunity to explore other perspectives and ways of doing things and should be considered informative. Note that some URLs contain a country extension, such as .au (Australia) or .se (Sweden), and may also include .gov, .org, and so on. A legitimate country extension in a URL should not be treated with suspicion. For instance, the Department of Statistics, South Africa can be found at a web address with the extension of .za (https://www.statssa.gov.za/).

★ Suspicious or fake domain extensions exist, so there are variants. Be cautious and investigate further before clicking on the site—for example, gooogle.com instead of google.com, or www.cdc.com instead of www.cdc.gov.

Read the "About Us" section:

★ While websites using .com can be legitimate, check the "About Us" page and use your judgment to assess how credible the source is.

★ Legitimate sources ideally include a contact page with an address, an email address, and often contact phone numbers.

★ Look for information about who the executives, staff members, and board members are. Their expertise in the field is vital for organizational credibility.

Check the dates:

★ Information can be old, but sometimes, information that seems old is the most current. This is sometimes the case when data are collected, and there is a lag time to process and make them available. Census data often fall into this category, as do data from trustworthy associations that only periodically collect information on a topic.

★ Follow up "old" data by searching Google to see whether there is anything more recent.

★ For online sources, check websites to determine whether the information is regularly updated. Most websites will be dated by either including a specific date the information was pulled together or having a copyright date.

★ The bottom line is to use the most recent data and cite your source when you use it. This will verify the currency of the information to others.

Follow up on the sources:

★ Ask whether the information cites well-respected sources that can be verified. And does the information come from research performed by qualified researchers? For instance, an item on the Commonwealth Fund website includes links to the original data or source.

★ When an article or website cites sources, look up those sources to be sure they are trustworthy. Sometimes, sources have official-sounding names but promote biased or fringe-view ideas.

★ If there are no sources cited, continue to familiarize yourself with the topic in other places to see whether what you are reading is accurate.

★ When you find something of interest and want to learn more, contact the author to discuss and elaborate on the work they are involved in. It is surprising how many authors are flattered and open to discussions.

Look for bias:

★ Think about whether the site has an agenda or mission that is furthered by sharing information and who is funding the source. Considering these will alert you to the biases that are inherent in the information.

★ Biased articles lean toward a particular point of view and try to persuade the reader toward a particular way of thinking. It can be intentional or unintentional.

★ Although not always transparent, consider whether the source has a vested interest in the information and how that might influence what is being communicated. For instance, consider the perspective or viewpoint of a lobby group sharing information. Organizations such as the National Rural Health Association (www.ruralhealth.us) have an interest in educating readers about the challenges and issues facing rural communities, which they do through well-documented research.

★ Is there a sense that information is missing? This can be intentional or unintentional. Consider also whether there are missing voices or voices that have been marginalized.

Think about credibility:

★ Blogs and web pages can be reliable but require further evaluation. These sites are quick and freely accessible ways to make information available. However, they may be biased and solely be the author's opinion.

★ Be skeptical of anything that is exaggerated, has a sensational tone, or seems illogical. If the information seems incredible or provocative, it may be a red flag to investigate the source further.

★ Exercise your discernment by considering the quality of the writing and editing. If there are frequent misspellings or grammatical errors, they are signs to be skeptical.

Websites Dedicated to Checking Facts

Reliable websites to fact-check information include these sites, and others can be found here: https://library.csi.cuny.edu/c.php?g=619342&p=4310783.

★ www.FactCheck.org is a project of the Annenberg Public Policy Center at the University of Pennsylvania. The site's mission is to "monitor the factual accuracy of what is said by major U.S. political figures."

★ www.snopes.com fact-checks the validity of articles found on social media and the internet. Each entry on the site lists the sources used for verification and the author's authority for reporting about the misinformation found in the article.

Staying Current with Information on Reliable Websites

When you find a website that you trust, there are ways to have the organization send you its latest information.

Many sources alert readers when new content and articles become available. Look around the site for "subscribe," "alerts," "email updates," or similar options. For instance, to keep abreast of the Agency for

Healthcare Research and Quality, head to their "Email Updates" page (https://subscriptions.ahrq.gov/accounts/USAHRQ/subscriber/new) and add your email address to get timely updates for your areas of interest. Others, such as KFF, have both an option to subscribe (https://www.kff.org/email/) and a "follow us" option (https://www.kff.org/follow-us/), allowing the reader to connect on a variety of social media platforms. Another example on the FierceHealthcare website (https://www.fiercehealthcare.com/) is a "subscribe" button prominently displayed at the top of the page.

The world abounds with biased, misleading, and altogether incorrect information, so use the criteria outlined to make informed decisions about the validity of your reading. Sharing accurate and timely information establishes your credibility. Along with what we have shared, you are also welcome to use the CRAAP test (Currency, Relevance, Authority, Accuracy, and Purpose), developed by California State University librarians to help determine whether sources are credible (https://library.csuchico.edu/sites/default/files/craap-test.pdf). This resource is designed with academics in mind, but the evaluation criteria are valuable for all.

ACKNOWLEDGMENTS

From the start, writing this book is about paying forward what I learned from my leadership experiences in the healthcare system industry. There are many people to whom I am grateful; however, a few stand out here.

Thank you to Ann Sheybani, a writing coach who, at the beginning, provided guidance on how to write a book. I know a lot about the healthcare system and its five sectors. However, writing a book was not my expertise, and Ann provided significant and valuable guidance.

To Janene Batten, who wrote the Appendix after I asked her to make this information available to the readers. Janene provided helpful editing and, of course, a perspective that I found important. Throughout my leadership time, I always needed information and data, and in writing this book, these websites, articles, and literature are critical for the readers.

Perspective is extremely important, and Jack Kennedy, an attorney, was a reader throughout the time I was writing this book. His practical and realistic advice and his role as an "intelligent general-ist" were extremely significant in keeping me away from insider talk and ensuring I was writing to a broader audience. Very, very helpful and necessary.

Jeff Amell was an insurance contact who checked in with me often enough to listen to my thoughts and provide feedback. Leadership requires listening to experts, and Jeff is an expert.

To Mark Gerzon, whose book I have read but whom I have never met and never heard speak. When I first came across his book and his systems thinking work, I knew immediately he was a significant world leader in making sustainable change. His work with the UN, the US Congress, and corporate and civic work is profound, and I was convinced of the practicality and reality of his model. Thank you, Mark Gerzon.

And now my colleagues, former students, friends with whom I have worked. I have learned from each one of you, and everything in this book reflects the times we worked together. Worked hard . . . because that is how you make change, lasting change. Thank you for all you have taught me.

Meir, thank you for your optimism and support.

Focused Determination.

ABOUT THE AUTHOR

Judith Kunisch is a seasoned healthcare strategist, leader, and educator whose expertise spans healthcare economics, executive leadership, and innovative service operations. She has worked in a variety of leadership roles alongside providers, payers, and policymakers on behalf of healthcare consumers and patients.

Kunisch has served as vice president of Medical Strategies for a Fortune 100 insurer working across the US; executive director of a for-profit managed care home network introducing full risk models in delivering care and working in partnership with several major insurance companies; and managing director of the not-for-profit Hartford Action Plan on Infant Health, bringing new models of preventive care to inner-city residents. Most recently, Kunisch led Yale University's Doctor of Nursing Practice (DNP) Healthcare Leadership program, where she mentored the next generation of healthcare leaders who worked as leaders in a wide variety of major US healthcare systems and who traveled to Yale monthly for seminars.

Kunisch has held influential positions on numerous governing boards, including the Donaghue Medical Research Foundation and Charter Oak FQHC, and she cofounded the Connecticut Partnership for Patient Safety, a public-private collaborative. As an expert panelist for the AHRQ Innovations Exchange, she worked with national leaders to advance healthcare service innovation and adoption across the US.

Her thought leadership extends to coauthoring peer-reviewed articles on infant mortality, healthcare marketing, and education, and presenting at national conferences. Recognized for her contributions, Kunisch has earned awards such as the Robert U. Massey, MD, Award for Distinguished Service and the T. Stewart Hamilton Fellowship for Healthcare Management.

A Six Sigma champion and member of Sigma Theta Tau Honor Society, Kunisch combines a passion for systemic change with decades of practical experience to inspire sustainable healthcare transformation.

REFERENCES

AAFP. (2015). *Rural practice, keeping physicians in (position paper)*. Retrieved March 24, 2024, from https://www.aafp.org/about/policies/all/rural-practice-keeping-physicians.html

Abelson, R. (2023, May 12). Corporate giants buy up primary care practices at rapid pace. *The New York Times*. Retrieved March 23, 2024, from https://www.nytimes.com/2023/05/08/health/primary-care-doctors-consolidation.html

Abramoff, M. D., Dai, T., & Zou, J. (2024). Scaling adoption of medical AI — Reimbursement from value-based care and fee-for-service perspectives. *NEJM AI*, *1*(5). https://doi.org/10.1056/AIpc2400083

Advisory Board. (2020). *CMS: US health care spending will reach $4T in 2020*. Retrieved March 17, 2024, from https://www.advisory.com/daily-briefing/2020/04/03/health-spending

Agency for Healthcare Research and Quality. (2022). *Patient centered medical home (PCMH)*. Retrieved March 24, 2024, from https://www.ahrq.gov/ncepcr/research/care-coordination/pcmh/index.html

American Academy of Actuaries. (2018, March). *Prescription drug spending in the U.S. health care system.* Retrieved March 31, 2024, from https://www. actuary.org/content/prescription-drug-spending-us-health-care-system

American Association of Colleges of Osteopathic Medicine. (n.d.). *U.S. colleges of osteopathic medicine.* Retrieved March 24, 2024, from https://www.aacom.org/become-a-doctor/prepare-for-medical-school/ us-colleges-of-osteopathic-medicine

American Hospital Association. (2023a). *Fact sheet: Hospital price transparency.* Retrieved May 12, 2024 from https://www.cms.gov/newsroom/ fact-sheets/hospital-price-transparency-fact-sheet

American Hospital Association. (2023b). *Setting the record straight: Private equity and health insurers acquire more physicians than hospitals.* Retrieved March 24, 2024, from https://www.aha.org/infographics/2023- 06-26-setting-record-straight-private-equity-and-health-insurers- acquire-more-physicians-hospitals

American Hospital Association. (2024). *Fast facts on U.S. hospitals, 2024.* Retrieved March 24, 2024, from https://www.aha.org/statistics/ fast-facts-us-hospitals

American Medical Association. (2023, March 13). *RVS update committee (RUC).* Retrieved March 17, 2024, from https://www.ama-assn.org/ about/rvs-update-committee-ruc/rvs-update-committee-ruc

Antono, B., Bazemore, A., Dankwa-Mullan, I., George, J., Jetty, A., Petterson, S., Rajmane, A., Rhee, K., Rosario, B. L., Scheufele, E., Willis, J., Robert Graham Center, American Board of Family Medicine, & IBM Watson Health. (2021). *Primary care in the United States: A chartbook of facts and statistics.* Retrieved July 22, 2024, from https:// www.graham-center.org/content/dam/rgc/documents/publications- reports/reports/PrimaryCareChartbook2021.pdf

Apple Inc. (2020). *Using Apple Watch for arrhythmia detection*. Retrieved March 31, 2024, from https://www.apple.com/healthcare/docs/site/Apple_Watch_Arrhythmia_Detection.pdf

Arias, E., Tejada-Vera, B., Ahmad, F., & Kochanek, K. D. (2021). *Provisional life expectancy estimates for 2020*. Retrieved March 2, 2024, from https://www.cdc.gov/nchs/data/vsrr/vsrr015-508.pdf

Arias, E., Xu, J., & Division of Vital Statistics. (2020, November 17). *United States life tables, 2018*. Retrieved March 2, 2024, from https://www.cdc.gov/nchs/data/nvsr/nvsr69/nvsr69-12-508.pdf

Assistant Secretary for Planning and Evaluation - Office of Science & Data Policy. (2002). *Issue brief: Trends in prescription drug spending, 2016–2021.*

Becker, M. M., & Mustafa, H. (2022). Retrenchment of Wisconsin's Well Woman Program and changes in insurance coverage around the Affordable Care Act. *Preventive Medicine Report, 30*(December), 101996. https://doi.org/10.1016/j.pmedr.2022.101996

Behm, C., Falvey, A., Hatton, R., & Portalatin, A. (2023). *100 largest hospitals and health systems in the US | 2023*. Beckers Hospital Review. Retrieved July 22, 2024, from https://www.beckershospitalreview.com/rankings-and-ratings/100-largest-hospitals-and-health-systems-in-the-us-2023.html

Berwick, D. M., Nolan, T. W., & Whittington, J. (2008). The triple aim: Care, health, and cost. *Health Affairs, 27*(3), 759–769. https://doi.org/10.1377/hlthaff.27.3.759

Biotechnology Innovation Organization. (2024). *About BIO*. Retrieved April 7, 2024, from https://www.bio.org/about

Bryan, H. (2022, January 19). *Venture capital 2021 recap—A record breaking year*. FactSet. Retrieved April 3, 2024, from https://insight.factset.com/venture-capital-2021-recap-a-record-breaking-year

Buolamwini, J. (2023). *Unmasking AI*. Random House.

Burkle, C. M. (2011). The advance of the retail health clinic market: The liability risk physicians may potentially face when supervising or collaborating with other professionals. *Mayo Clinic Proceedings, 86*(11), 1086–1091. https://doi.org/10.4065/mcp.2011.0291

Burton, H. M. (2022). *Systems thinking for beginners: Learn the essential systems thinking skills to navigate an increasingly complex world for effective problem solving and decision.* Independently published.

Cambridge Dictionary. (2024). Dynamics. In *Cambridge Dictionary.* https://dictionary.cambridge.org/us/dictionary/english/dynamics

Camillus, J. C. (2008). Strategy as a wicked problem. *Harvard Business Review, 86*(5), 98–106+130. https://www.scopus.com/inward/record.uri?eid=2-s2.0-43949105194&partnerID=40&md5=6422b58b06f62c852eacdf2c4bbe4ff0

Centers for Disease Control and Prevention. (2021). *The U.S. Public Health Service untreated syphilis study at Tuskegee: Research implications.* Retrieved March 31, 2024, from https://www.cdc.gov/tuskegee/after.htm

CMS.gov. (n.d.-a). *Assessing equity to drive health care improvements: Learnings from the CMS Innovation Center.* Retrieved May 12, 2024, from https://www.cms.gov/priorities/innovation/data-and-reports/2023/assessing-equity-hc-improv-wp

CMS.gov. (n.d.-b). *National health expenditures 2022 highlights.* Retrieved March 24, 2024, from https://www.cms.gov/files/document/highlights.pdf

CMS.gov. (2022, March 18). *CMS Office of the Actuary releases 2021–2030 projections of national health expenditures.* https://www.cms.gov/newsroom/press-releases/cms-office-actuary-releases-2021-2030-projections-national-health-expenditures

CMS.gov. (2023a). *Health Information Technology for Economic and Clinical Health (HITECH) audits.* Retrieved March 31, 2024, from https://www.cms.gov/medicare/audits-compliance/part-a-cost-report/health-information-technology-economic-and-clinical-health-hitech-audits

CMS.gov. (2023b). *Hospital price transparency.* Retrieved May 12, 2024, from https://www.cms.gov/priorities/key-initiatives/hospital-price-transparency#:~:text=Hospital%20Price%20Transparency-,Hospital%20Price%20Transparency,or%20service%20before%20receiving%20it

CMS.gov. (2023c). *Medical loss ratio.* Retrieved March 17, 2024, from https://www.cms.gov/marketplace/private-health-insurance/medical-loss-ratio

CMS.gov. (2023d). *NHE fact sheet.* Retrieved March 17, 2024, from https://www.cms.gov/Research-Statistics-Data-and-Systems/Statistics-Trends-and-Reports/NationalHealthExpendData/NHE-Fact-Sheet

CMS.gov. (2023e). *Projected.* Retrieved May 20, 2024, from https://www.cms.gov/data-research/statistics-trends-and-reports/national-health-expenditure-data/projected

CMS.gov. (2023f). *What are the value-based programs?* Retrieved May 2, 2024, from https://www.cms.gov/medicare/quality/value-based-programs

CMS.gov. (2023, September 6). *Mandatory insurer reporting for group health plans (GHP).* https://www.cms.gov/medicare/coordination-benefits-recovery/mandatory-insurer-reporting-group-health-plans

CMS.gov. (2024, January 29). *Participation continues to grow in CMS' accountable care organization initiatives in 2024.* https://www.cms.gov/newsroom/press-releases/participation-continues-grow-cms-account-able-care-organization-initiatives-2024

CMS.gov. (2024, March 15). *Overview of rules & fact sheets.* Retrieved March 17, 2024, from https://www.cms.gov/nosurprises/policies-and-resources/overview-of-rules-fact-sheets

Collins Higgins, T., Babalola, E., Crosson, J., Mathematica Policy Research, & Agency for Healthcare Research and Quality. (2015). *Primary care practice facilitation curriculum. Module 3: The primary care landscape.* https://www.ahrq.gov/sites/default/files/wysiwyg/ncepcr/tools/PCMH/pcpf-module-3-primary-care-landscape.pdf

Commonwealth Fund. (2023, February 7). *Value-based care: What it is, and why it's needed.* Retrieved May 15, 2024, from https://www.commonwealthfund.org/publications/explainer/2023/feb/value-based-care-what-it-is-why-its-needed

Commonwealth Fund. (2023, October 26). *Paying for it: How health care costs and medical debt are making Americans sicker and poorer.* Retrieved March 11, 2024, from https://www.commonwealthfund.org/publications/surveys/2023/oct/paying-for-it-costs-debt-americans-sicker-poorer-2023-affordability-survey?utm_campaign=Achieving%20Universal%20Coverage&utm_medium=email&_hsmi=279980337&_hsenc=p2ANqtz-_G9LZUtVaqmdAXozMdqLNwSubzagSQPR5N-pIZFokPsw1Ll5ulr4QumLsN7eZufuhsSYl8Q_8IXzKGgWjOpfOgYZe2uan06oTeurjQIl0I6PUm42m8&utm_source=alert

Congressional Budget Office. (2021, April 8). *Research and development in the pharmaceutical industry.* Retrieved March 31, 2024, from www.cbo.gov/publication/57025

Congressional Budget Office. (2024, March 5). *The federal budget in fiscal year 2023: An infographic.* Retrieved April 7, 2024, from https://www.cbo.gov/publication/59727#:~:text=The%20federal%20deficit%20in%202023,percent%20of%20gross%20domestic%20product

Congressional Research Service. (2017, November 17). *Congressional commissions: Overview, structure, and legislative considerations.* Retrieved

April 7, 2024, from https://crsreports.congress.gov/product/pdf/R/R40076/18

Consumer Financial Protection Bureau. (2022, March 1). *Medical debt burden in the United States.* Retrieved March 11, 2024, from https://www.consumerfinance.gov/data-research/research-reports/medical-debt-burden-in-the-united-states/

Cubanski, J., Fuglesten Biniek, J., & Neuman, T. (2023, March 20). *FAQs on health spending, the federal budget, and budget enforcement tools.* KFF. Retrieved March 17, 2024, from https://www.kff.org/medicare/issue-brief/faqs-on-health-spending-the-federal-budget-and-budget-enforcement-tools/

Cubanski, J., Neuman, T., & Freed, M. (2024, January 24). *Explaining the prescription drug provisions in the Inflation Reduction Act.* KFF. Retrieved April 7, 2024, from https://www.kff.org/medicare/issue-brief/explaining-the-prescription-drug-provisions-in-the-inflation-reduction-act/

Donahoe, G. F. (2021). *Estimates of medical device spending in the United States.* Retrieved April 3, 2024, from https://www.advamed.org/wp-content/uploads/2021/12/Estimates-Medical-Device-Spending-United-States-Report-2021.pdf

Duke University School of Medicine. (2024). *Michael Pencina, PhD.* Retrieved June 15, 2024, from https://medschool.duke.edu/personnel/michael-pencina-phd

Ervin, S. M. (2017). History of nursing education in the United States. In S. B. Keating & S. De Boor (Eds.), *Curricular development and evaluation in nursing education* (4th ed.). Springer Publications.

Evans, M. (2022, June 12). The billionaire funding a battle against hospital monopolies. *The Wall Street Journal.* https://www.wsj.com/articles/the-billionaire-funding-a-battle-against-hospital-monopolies-11654920006

Evans, M. (2024, March 26). Patients rack up hidden hospital fees. *The Wall Street Journal*, A3.

Evans, M., & Weil, J. (2024, March 21). A Bat Infestation, Postponed Surgeries and Unpaid Bills: A Hospital Chain in Crisis. *The Wall Street Journal*. https://www.wsj.com/health/healthcare/hospital-chain-financial-crisis-steward-mpt-45be8bfb?st=MvMX1d&reflink=article_

FQHC Associates. (n.d.). *What is an FQHC?* Retrieved April 7, 2024, from https://www.fqhc.org/what-is-an-fqhc

Frieden, T. (2022, March 25). Stopping a pandemic deadlier than covid. *The Wall Street Journal*. https://www.wsj.com/articles/stopping-a-pandemic-deadlier-than-covid-11648220259?page=1

Garber, J. (2023, April 28). *5 things you need to know about hospital community benefit spending*. Lown Institute. Retrieved May 15, 2024, from https://lowninstitute.org/5-things-you-need-to-know-about-hospital-community-benefit-spending/

Gerzon, M. (2006). *Leading through conflict: How successful leaders transform differences into opportunities*. Harvard Business School Press.

Gonzalez, G., & Becker's Hospital Review. (2022, June 13). *This billionaire is pushing back against hospital monopolies*. Retrieved March 24, 2024 from https://www.beckershospitalreview.com/hospital-management-administration/this-billionaire-is-pushing-back-against-hospital-monopolies.html

Gooch, K. (2022, April 19). *74% of physicians are hospital or corporate employees, with pandemic fueling increase*. Becker's Hospital Review. Retrieved March 24, 2024, from https://www.beckershospitalreview.com/hospital-physician-relationships/74-of-physicians-are-hospital-or-corporate-employees-with-pandemic-fueling-increase.html

Google Fitbit. (n.d.). *Information we collect*. Retrieved March 31, 2024, from https://www.fitbit.com/global/us/legal/privacy-policy#info-we-collect

Grassley, C. (2023). *Senate budget committee digs into impact of private equity ownership in America's hospitals.* Retrieved March 24, 2024, from https://www.grassley.senate.gov/news/news-releases/senate-budget-committee-digs-into-impact-of-private-equity-ownership-in-americas-hospitals

Gunja, M. Z., Gumas, E. D., & Williams, R. D. (2023, January 31). *U.S. health care from a global perspective, 2022: Accelerating spending, worsening outcomes.* The Commonwealth Fund. Retrieved March 18, 2024, from https://www.commonwealthfund.org/publications/issue-briefs/2023/jan/us-health-care-global-perspective-2022

Haendel, M., Vasilevsky, N., Unni, D., Bologa, C., Harris, N., Rehm, H., Hamosh, A., Baynam, G., Groza, T., McMurry, J., Dawkins, H., Rath, A., Thaxton, C., Bocci, G., Joachimiak, M. P., Köhler, S., Robinson, P. N., Mungall, C., & Oprea, T. I. (2020). How many rare diseases are there? *Nature Reviews Drug Discovery, 19*(2), 77–78. https://doi.org/10.1038/d41573-019-00180-y

Hart, A. (2024, February 6). *Is housing health care? State Medicaid programs increasingly say 'yes'.* KFF Health News. Retrieved May 12, 2024, from https://kffhealthnews.org/news/article/housing-homeless-medicaid-supports-waivers-health-insurance/

Health Resources & Services Administration. (n.d.). *Hill–Burton free and reduced-cost healthcare.* Retrieved March 9, 2024, from https://www.hrsa.gov/get-health-care/affordable/hill-burton

Healthgrades for Professionals. (2023). *The 10 largest health systems in the US.* Retrieved July 22, 2024, from https://www.healthgrades.com/pro/the-10-largest-health-systems-in-the-us

Heiss, R. (2020). Fighting health infodemics: The role of citizen empowerment. *Eurohealth 26*(3). https://iris.who.int/bitstream/handle/10665/338919/Eurohealth-26-3-23-25-eng.pdf

Hernandez, I., & Hung, A. (2024). A primer on brand-name prescription drug reimbursement in the United States. *Journal of Managed Care & Specialty Pharmacy, 30*(1), 99–106. https://doi.org/10.18553/jmcp.2024.30.1.99

Hood, L., & Price, N. (2023, March 25). The AI will see you now. *The Wall Street Journal.*

Horstman, C. (2023, August 15). *Promoting health equity by changing how we pay for care.* The Commonwealth Fund. Retrieved May 12, 2024, from https://www.commonwealthfund.org/blog/2023/promoting-health-equity-changing-how-we-pay-care

Hostetter, M., Klein, S., Commonwealth Fund, & Bassett Research Institute. (2023). *How regional partnerships bolster rural hospitals.*

HRSA. (2023). *Health workforce: National Center for Health Workforce Analysis November 2023.*

Insurance Matters to CT. (2021). *Get the facts.* Retrieved March 17, 2024, from https://insurancematterstoct.com/get-the-facts/

International Medical Aid. (2023). *How many medical schools in US: The definitive guide (2024).* Retrieved March 24, 2024, from https://medicalaid.org/how-many-medical-schools-in-us-the-definitive-guide-2023/

Investopedia Team. (n.d.). *Which industry spends the most on lobbying?* Investopedia. Retrieved March 11, 2024, from https://www.investopedia.com/investing/which-industry-spends-most-lobbying-antm-so/

Jamble, R. (2024, February 19). *Ultimate list of top EMR systems.* SelectHub. Retrieved March 31, 2024, from https://www.selecthub.com/medical-software/popular-emr-ehr-software-list/

Joint Commission. (n.d.). *R3 report issue 36: New requirements to reduce health care disparities.* Retrieved May 12, 2024, from https://www.

jointcommission.org/standards/r3-report/r3-report-issue-36-new-requirements-to-reduce-health-care-disparities/

Joint Commission. (2023, August 16). *The Joint Commission and National Quality Forum join forces to improve healthcare quality, safety, equity, and value.* Retrieved May 12, 2024, from https://www.jointcommission.org/resources/news-and-multimedia/news/2023/08/joint-commission-and-national-quality-forum-join-forces/

Kaiser Permanente. (2023). *How Kaiser Permanente evolved.* Retrieved March 2, 2024, from https://about.kaiserpermanente.org/who-we-are/our-history/how-it-all-started

Karpman, M., Martinchek, K., & Braga, B. (2022, May 11). *Medical debt fell during the pandemic. How can the decline be sustained?* Urban Institute. Retrieved March 11, 2024, from https://www.urban.org/research/publication/medical-debt-fell-during-pandemic-how-can-decline-be-sustained

Keehan, S. P., Fiore, J. A., Poisal, J. A., Cuckler, G. A., Sisko, A. M., Smith, S. D., Madison, A. J., & Rennie, K. E. (2023). National health expenditure projections, 2022–31: Growth to stabilize once the COVID-19 public health emergency ends. *Health Affairs, 42*(7), 886–898. https://doi.org/10.1377/hlthaff.2023.00403

KFF. (2022). *Health insurance coverage of the total population.* Retrieved March 9, 2024, from https://www.kff.org/other/state-indicator/total-population/?currentTimeframe=0&sortModel=%7B%22colId%22:%22Location%22,%22sort%22:%22asc%22%7D

Kohane, I. S. (2023). Injecting artificial intelligence into medicine. *NEJM AI, 1*(1). https://doi.org/10.1056/AIe2300197

Kunisch, J. (1989). Electronic fetal monitors: Marketing forces and the resulting controversy. In K. Ratcliff (Ed.), *Healing technology: Feminist perspectives*, 41-60. University of Michigan Press.

Landi, H. (2024, April 3). *Epic plans to launch AI validation software for healthcare organizations to test, monitor models.* Fierce Healthcare. https://www.fiercehealthcare.com/ai-and-machine-learning/epic-plans-launch-ai-validation-software-healthcare-organizations-test

Lee, V. S. (2020). *The long fix: Solving America's health care crisis with strategies that work for everyone.* W. W. Norton & Company.

Lejeune, A., Le Glaz, A., Perron, P. A., Sebti, J., Baca-Garcia, E., Walter, M., Lemey, C., & Berrouiguet, S. (2022). Artificial intelligence and suicide prevention: A systematic review. *European Psychiatry, 65*(1), article e19. https://doi.org/10.1192/j.eurpsy.2022.8

Leonard, F., Jacobson, G., Haynes, L. A., Collins, S. R., & (2022, October 17). *Traditional Medicare or Medicare Advantage: How older Americans choose and why.* The Commonwealth Fund. Retrieved March 2, 2024, from https://www.commonwealthfund.org/publications/issue-briefs/2022/oct/traditional-medicare-or-advantage-how-older-americans-choose

Lindwall, C. (2024, January 19). *The latest in Apple's patent dispute over the Ultra 2 and Series 9 smartwatches.* Retrieved April 4, 2024, from https://www.consumerreports.org/electronics-computers/smartwatch/apple-patent-dispute-ultra-2-series-9-smartwatches-a4679851226/#:~:text=In%20October%2C%20the%20ITC%20found,technology%20company%20based%20in%20California

Lukens, G. (2023, September 12). *Analyzing the Census Bureau's 2022 poverty, income, and health insurance data.* Center on Budget and Policy Priorities. https://www.cbpp.org/blog/analyzing-the-census-bureaus-2022-poverty-income-and-health-insurance-data#Gideon-220PM

Mackintosh, J. (2023, November 1). Streetwise: This correction is so confusing. *The Wall Street Journal,* B1. https://global.factiva.com/ga/default.aspx?page_driver=searchBuilder_Search&

Magee, M. (2019). *Code blue: Inside America's medical industrial complex.* Atlantic Monthly Press.

McGough, M., Winger, A., Kurani, N. & Cox, C. (2023, October 7). *Health spending: How much is health spending expected to grow?* Peterson-KFF Health System Tracker. Retrieved March 4, 2024, from https://www.healthsystemtracker.org/chart-collection/how-much-is-health-spending-expected-to-grow/#Annual%20change%20in%20per%20capita%20health%20spending,%201970s%20%E2%80%93%202021;%20projected%202022%20%E2%80%93%202031

Meadows, D. H. (2008). *Thinking in systems: A primer.* Chelsea Green Publishing.

Melnyk, B. M., Fineout-Overholt, E., Stillwell, S. B., & Williamson, K. M. (2010). Evidence-based practice: Step by step: The seven steps of evidence-based practice. *American Journal of Nursing, 110*(1), 51–53. https://doi.org/10.1097/01.NAJ.0000366056.06605.d2

Merriam-Webster. (1981). Industry. In *Webster's Third New International Dictionary of the English Language* (pp. 1155–1156).

Moore, C. (n.d.). *Q4'23 global VC deals volume drops to level not seen since Q3'16.* KPMG. Retrieved April 3, 2024, from https://kpmg.com/xx/en/home/media/press-releases/2024/01/q4-2023-global-vc-deals-volume-drops-to-level-not-seen-since-q3-2016.html

Muhammad, M. (2023). *Health systems in 10 years: 20 predictions from top executives.* Becker's Hospital Review. Retrieved June 21, 2024, from https://www.beckershospitalreview.com/strategy/health-systems-in-10-years-20-predictions-from-top-executives.html?origin=CIOE&utm_source=CIOE&utm_medium=email&utm_content=newsletter&oly_enc_id=9296C9303267E6D

National WWII Museum. (n.d.). *The Nuremberg trials.* Retrieved March 31, 2024, from https://www.nationalww2museum.org/war/topics/nuremberg-trials

Navathe, A. S., & Liao, J. M. (2022, August 15). *Viewpoint: Aligning value-based payments with health equity. A framework for reforming payment reforms*. JAMA Network. https://jamanetwork.com/journals/jama/fullarticle/2795498

Neuwirth, Z. E. (2019). *Reframing healthcare: A roadmap for creating disruptive change*. Advantage Media Group.

NRHA. (n.d.). *About NHRA*. Retrieved March 24, 2024, from https://www.ruralhealth.us/about-nrha/about-rural-health-care

OpenSecrets. (2024). *Industries*. Retrieved April 7, 2024, from https://www.opensecrets.org/federal-lobbying/industries

Pearl, R. (2021). *Uncaring: How the culture of medicine kills doctors & patients*. Hatchett Book Group.

Pearl, R. (2024). *Medical malpractice in the age of AI: Who will bear the blame?* TwinCities. Retrieved June 1, 2024, from https://www.twincities.com/2024/05/30/robert-pearl-medical-malpractice-in-the-age-of-ai-who-will-bear-the-blame/

Pearl, R. (2024, March 25). *3 ways ChatGPT's new 'memory' can transform healthcare*. LinkedIn. Retrieved March 31, 2024, from https://www.linkedin.com/pulse/3-ways-chatgpts-new-memory-can-transform-healthcare-pearl-m-d--udvbc/

Peterson-KFF Health System Tracker. (2024). *Percent uninsured*. Retrieved July 22, 242, from https://www.healthsystemtracker.org/indicator/access-affordability/percent-uninsured/#Percent%20of%20uninsured%20adults,%20by%20age,%202022

Physicians Advocacy Institute. (2022). *COVID-19's impact on acquisitions of physician practices and physician employment 2019–2021*. Retrieved March 24, 2024, from https://www.physiciansadvocacyinstitute.org/Portals/0/assets/docs/PAI-Research/PAI%20Avalere%20Physician%20Employment%20Trends%20Study%202019-21%20Final.pdf?ver=ksWkgjKXB_yZfImFdXlvGg%3d%3d

Poisal, J. A., Sisko, A. M., Cuckler, G. A., Smith, S. D., Keehan, S. P., Fiore, J. A., Madison, A. J., & Rennie, K. E. (2022). National health expenditure projections, 2021–30: Growth to moderate as COVID-19 impacts wane. *Health Affairs, 41*(4), 474–486. https://doi.org/10.1377/hlthaff.2022.00113

Porter, M. E., & Olmsted Teisber, E. (2006). *Redefining health care: Creating value-based competition on results.* Harvard Business School Press.

Radley, D. C., Shah, A., Collins, S. R., Powe, N. R., & Zephyrin, L. C. (2024). *Advancing racial equity in U.S. health care: The Commonwealth Fund 2024 state health disparities report.* The Commonwealth Fund. Retrieved May 12, 2024, from https://www.commonwealthfund.org/publications/fund-reports/2024/apr/advancing-racial-equity-us-health-care

Rau, J. (2023, August 3). *Look up your hospital: Is it being penalized by Medicare?* KFF Health News. Retrieved May 2, 2024, from https://kffhealthnews.org/news/hospital-penalties/

Ready, D., Salazar, J., & Verboon, C. (2023). *The federal budget in fiscal year 2023.* Congressional Budget Office. Retrieved April 7, 2024, from https://www.cbo.gov/system/files/2024-03/59727-Federal-Budget.pdf

Reed, T. (2023, November 7). *U.S. health outcomes worse than OECD nations on most measures.* Axios. Retrieved July 22, 2024, from https://www.axios.com/2023/11/07/us-health-gdp-oecd#

Reinhardt, U. E. (2013). *Statement by Uwe E. Reinhardt before the hearing on "30 million new patients and 11 months to go: Who will provide their primary care?"* Retrieved April 28, 2024, from https://www.help.senate.gov/imo/media/doc/Reinhardt.pdf

Research!America. (2022, January). *U.S. investments in medical and health research and development: 2016–2020.* Retrieved April 7, 2024, from https://www.researchamerica.org/wp-content/uploads/2022/09/ResearchAmerica-Investment-Report.Final_.January-2022-1.pdf

RevCycleIntelligence. (n.d.). *The role of the hospital charge-master in revenue cycle management.* Retrieved March 24, 2024, from https://revcycleintelligence.com/features/the-role-of-the-hospital-chargemaster-in-revenue-cycle-management

RHIhub. (2023). *Critical access hospitals (CAHs).* Retrieved March 24, 2024, from https://www.ruralhealthinfo.org/topics/critical-access-hospitals

Rice, D. P., & Cooper, B. S. (1970). *National health expenditures, 1929-6.* Retrieved April 3, 2024, from https://www.ssa.gov/policy/docs/ssb/v33n1/v33n1p3.pdf

Rosenberg, C. (2020. May 7). *Relics of the infectious past: Disease warning signs collection.* Circulating Now. https://circulatingnow.nlm.nih.gov/2020/05/07/relics-of-the-infectious-past-disease-warning-sign-collection/

Schneider, E. C., Sarnak, D. O., Squires, D., Shah, A., & Doty, M. M. (n.d.). *Mirror, mirror 2017: International comparison reflects flaws and opportunities for better U.S. health care.* The Commonwealth Fund. Retrieved July 22, 2024, from https://interactives.commonwealthfund.org/2017/july/mirror-mirror/

Smith, S., & Blank, A. (2023). *Spotlight on statistics: Healthcare occupations: Characteristics of the employed.* U.S. Bureau of Labor Statistics. Retrieved March 2, 2024, from https://www.bls.gov/spotlight/2023/healthcare-occupations-in-2022/home.htm

State of the primary care workforce, 2023. Retrieved July 22, 2024, from https://bhw.hrsa.gov/sites/default/files/bureau-health-workforce/data-research/state-of-primary-care-workforce-2023.pdf

Strain, T., Wijndaele, K., & Brage, S. (2019). Physical activity surveillance through smartphone apps and wearable trackers: Examining the UK potential for nationally representative sampling. *JMIR mHealth and uHealth, 7*(1), article e11898. https://doi.org/10.2196/11898

Thomas, D., & Wessel, C. (2023, June). *The state of emerging therapeutic companies*. Biotechnology Innovation Organization. Retrieved March 31, 2024, from https://www.bio.org/sites/default/files/2023-06/State_of_Industry_Report_v2.pdf

Tison, G. H., Sanchez, J. M., Ballinger, B., Singh, A., Olgin, J. E., Pletcher, M. J., Vittinghoff, E., Lee, E. S., Fan, S. M., Gladstone, R. A., Mikell, C., Sohoni, N., Hsieh, J., & Marcus, G. M. (2018). Passive detection of atrial fibrillation using a commercially available smartwatch. *JAMA Cardiology*, *3*(5), 409–416. https://doi.org/10.1001/jamacardio.2018.0136

Toussaint, J. S. (2021, January 6). *Why Haven Healthcare failed*. Harvard Business Review. Retrieved May 12, 2024, from https://hbr.org/2021/01/why-haven-healthcare-failed

U.S. Bureau of Labor Statistics. (2020). *Registered nurses made up 30 percent of hospital employment in May 2019*. Retrieved March 24, 2024, from https://www.bls.gov/opub/ted/2020/registered-nurses-made-up-30-percent-of-hospital-employment-in-may-2019.htm

U.S. Const. art. 1, §8: Powers of Congress.

U.S. Const. pmbl. (1787).

U.S. Department of Health and Human Services. (2022). *The Belmont report*. Retrieved March 31, 2024, from https://www.hhs.gov/ohrp/regulations-and-policy/belmont-report/index.html

U.S. Food & Drug Administration. (2024). *Artificial intelligence and medical products: How CBER, CDER, CDRH, and OCP are working together*. Retrieved June 15, 2024, from https://www.fda.gov/medical-devices/software-medical-device-samd/artificial-intelligence-and-machine-learning-software-medical-device#:~:text=The%20FDA's%20traditional%20paradigm%20of,may%20need%20a%20premarket%20review

United States Senate Committee on the Budget. (2023). *Senate Budget Committee digs into impact of private equity ownership in America's hospitals*. Retrieved March 24, 2024, from https://www.budget.senate. gov/chairman/newsroom/press/senate-budget-committee-digs-into-impact-of-private-equity-ownership-in-americas-hospitals

US Inflation Calculator. (2024). *Health care inflation in the United States (1948–2024)*. https://www.usinflationcalculator.com/inflation/ health-care-inflation-in-the-united-states/

USF Health. (n.d.). *Health informatics*. Retrieved March 31, 2024, from https://www.usfhealthonline.com/areas-of-study/health-informatics/

VanHouten, J. P., & Brandt, C. A. (2021, July 7). Universal patient identification: What it is and why the US needs it. *Health Affairs*. Retrieved March 9, 2024, from https://www.healthaffairs.org/content/forefront/ universal-patient-identification-and-why-us-needs

Voltz, D. (2024). OpenAI's Sam Altman and other tech leaders to serve on AI safety board. *The Wall Street Journal*, A3. https://www.wsj.com/ tech/ai/openais-sam-altman-and-other-tech-leaders-to-serve-on-ai-safety-board-7dc47b78

Walker, J. (2023, November 22). Senators call for investigation of health insurers' role in driving up drug costs. *The Wall Street Journal*.

Warner, J. J., Benjamin, I. J., Churchwell, K., Firestone, G., Gardner, T. J., Johnson, J. C., Ng-Osorio, J., Rodriguez, C. J., Todman, L., Yaffe, K., Yancy, C. W., & Harrington, R. A.. (2020). Advancing healthcare reform: The American Heart Association's 2020 statement of principles for adequate, accessible, and affordable health care: A presidential advisory from the American Heart Association. *Circulation*, *141*(10), e601–e614. https://doi.org/10.1161/CIR.0000000000000759

Whyte, L. E. (2023). New health research agency, ARPA-H, starts search for two hub locations. *The Wall Street Journal*. https://global.factiva.com/ ga/default.aspx?page_driver=searchBuilder_Search&

Williams, E., Rudowitz, R., & Burns, A. (2023). *Medicaid financing: The basics*. KFF. Retrieved March 2, 2024, from https://www.kff.org/medicaid/issue-brief/medicaid-financing-the-basics/

World Bank Group. (2015). *Public-private partnerships*. Retrieved May 2, 2024, from https://www.worldbank.org/en/news/video/2015/05/05/public-private-partnerships#:~:text=PPPs%20are%20a%20way%20of,What%20are%20they%20not%3F

Yearby, R., Clark, B., & Figueroa, J. F. (2022). Structural racism in historical and modern US health care policy. *Health Affairs*, *41*(2). https://doi.org/10.1377/hlthaff.2021.01466

www.ingramcontent.com/pod-product-compliance
Lightning Source LLC
Chambersburg PA
CBHW031924190326
41519CB00007B/410